Praise for
The Truth About Starting a Business

"When thinking about starting a business, have you ever felt discouraged because you did not know somebody or some thing? If that is the case, Barringer can be your wise uncle. In this insightful new book, he shares common-sense advice, based on research that can help to get you started and going in the right direction to launch your own venture."

James Fiet, Ph.D., Brown Forman Chair in Entrepreneurship,
University of Louisville

"Relevant and easily accessible advice on how to start your own business. Barringer's great primer covers it all, from naming your company to handling legalities, from publicity to the psychology of being an entrepreneur."

Matt Hedges, Founder and President,
Vino de Sol

"This book is a must read! Barringer has developed an easy-to-follow blueprint on how to start a new business. He takes the complexity of entrepreneurship and streamlines it, providing insight and expertise that is invaluable to those venturing out on their own."

Christopher Jones, CAGS, Licensed Educational Psychologies, NCSP,
President & CEO, Dynamic Interventions, Inc.

"I found myself smiling as I read some of the truths because I found it talking about myself and peers who have started numerous companies. This book should be on the seasoned entrepreneur's list of 'what I should have read before I started my business.'"

Joe Keeley, President & CEO,
College Nannies & Tutors Development

"This book is the ultimate handbook for starting a business: from coming up with an idea to implementing it with success and vigor. It walks a potential business owner through the steps of writing a business plan, creating an identity, financing a business, hiring personnel, marketing, and creating a work-life balance. It is a tool that no new business owner should be without."

Dr. Emily Levy, Founder & CEO,
EBL Coaching

"Barringer cuts to the chase with his simple, relevant, and hard-hitting truths. In practical language and with significant insight about the realities of venture start-up, he speaks on very personal level to the prospective entrepreneur."

Michael H. Morris, PhD, Chris J. Witting Chair and Professor,
Whitman School of Management, Syracuse University

THE TRUTH ABOUT

STARTING A BUSINESS

Bruce R. Barringer

© 2009 by Pearson Education, Inc.
Publishing as FT Press
Upper Saddle River, New Jersey 07458

FT Press offers excellent discounts on this book when ordered in quantity for bulk purchases or special sales. For more information, please contact U.S. Corporate and Government Sales, 1-800-382-3419, corpsales@pearsontechgroup.com. For sales outside the U.S., please contact International Sales at international@pearsoned.com.

Printed in the United States of America

Printed in the United States of America

First Printing December 2008

ISBN-10: 0-13-714450-4
ISBN-13: 978-0-13-714450-1

Pearson Education LTD.
Pearson Education Australia PTY, Limited.
Pearson Education Singapore, Pte. Ltd.
Pearson Education North Asia, Ltd.
Pearson Education Canada, Ltd.
Pearson Educatión de Mexico, S.A. de C.V.
Pearson Education—Japan
Pearson Education Malaysia, Pte. Ltd.

Library of Congress Cataloging-in-Publication Data

Barringer, Bruce R.

The truth about starting a business / Bruce Barringer.

p. cm.

ISBN 0-13-714450-4 (pbk. : alk. paper) 1. New business enterprises. 2. Entrepreneurship. 3. Small business. I. Title.

HD62.5.B365 2008

658.1'1--dc22

2008028521

Vice President, Publisher
Tim Moore

Associate Publisher and Director of Marketing
Amy Neidlinger

Acquisitions Editor
Jennifer Simon

Editorial Assistant
Pamela Boland

Development Editor
Russ Hall

Operations Manager
Gina Kanouse

Digital Marketing Manager
Julie Phifer

Publicity Manager
Laura Czaja

Assistant Marketing Manager
Megan Colvin

Marketing Assistant
Brandon Smith

Cover and Interior Designs
Stuart Jackman, Dorling Kindersley

Design Manager
Sandra Schroeder

Managing Editor
Kristy Hart

Senior Project Editor
Lori Lyons

Copy Editor
Karen A. Gill

Proofreader
San Dee Phillips

Senior Compositor
Gloria Schurick

Manufacturing Buyer
Dan Uhrig

Part VI The Truth About Building a New Business Team

Part VII The Truth About Intellectual Property

Part VIII The Truth About Marketing

Part IX The Truth About Financial Management

Part X The Truth About Growing a Business

Part XI The Truth About Starting a Business and Maintaining a Healthy Personal Life

TRUTH

1

Why people start businesses

You're flipping through a magazine and come across a test that assesses whether you have the right personality to start a business. You take the test and learn that you're best suited for a traditional career. Your heart sinks, because you've been giving business ownership some thought. But you figure that the people who designed the test know what they're doing. Right? Wrong!

There's no scientific evidence that shows that people with certain personalities are more likely to start a business or will be a more successful business owner than anyone else. In fact, the somewhat surprising collection of research results illustrate that there are no meaningful differences between business owners and nonbusiness owners on the most basic human characteristics, behaviors, and desires.[1] Most people, for example, want to make more money and crave independence, not just business owners. People who start their own businesses are just as diverse as people in regular jobs. You don't have to have a certain personality, behave in a particular way, or have a certain set of desires to be a successful business owner.

> You don't have to have a certain personality, behave in a particular way, or have a certain set of desires to be a successful business owner.

What, then, motivates people to start their own business? In most instances, it's riskier and harder to start and run a business than it is to traverse a traditional career. Although there are many reasons that motivate people to start their own business, two reasons are paramount: the presence of aspiration gaps in people's lives, and passion for a business idea.

Aspiration gaps

All of us have aspirations, which are made up of our most important goals, objectives, ambitions, and longings. Our aspirations vary because they're influenced by our values, abilities, experiences, families, and individual circumstances. When one or more of our aspirations are unmet, we have aspiration gaps in our lives.

Collectively, our aspirations form what researchers call our aspiration vectors. Sometimes our aspirations vectors get complex, like when we're simultaneously trying to build a career, raise kids, love our spouse, save money, and so on. For people who have strong aspirations and are insistent that certain aspirations are met, their aspirations become the driving force in their lives. For example, a young mother might have the following three aspirations: a job that pays at least $35,000 per year, the ability to be home by 3:00 p.m. on weekdays to meet the school bus, and Sundays free to participate in church and volunteer-related activities. Similarly, the assistant manager for a large retail chain, like Home Depot or Target, might be driven by the single aspiration to have his own store by the time he is 30.

People can become discouraged or distressed when they look at their job or alternative jobs in the traditional labor market and conclude that none of the choices will allow their most important aspirations to be met. In these instances, an alternative is to start a business. Although starting a business isn't easier than a traditional job, business owners usually have more discretion and control over their schedule and career trajectory. This discretion and control helps people better juggle both professional and family-related goals and aspirations and accomplish the things they want the most.[2]

Passion for a business idea

A second factor that motivates people to start their own businesses is passion for a business idea. What frequently happens is that a person gets an idea for a new product or service, and there is no practical way to bring the idea to market other than starting a new business. In these instances, a person's passion for the idea is determined by how desirable and feasible the idea seems to be.[3] Many prospective business owners become very passionate about their ideas,

Small business owners often work long hours and make sacrifices to make their businesses work, but they say it's worth it because they're passionate about the businesses they're running.

particularly if they believe that the resulting business will improve their own circumstances and positively influence other people's lives.

An important result of passion is that it often elicits extraordinary effort on the part of business owners to get their businesses off the ground and to run them successfully. Small business owners often work long hours and make sacrifices to make their businesses work, but they say it's worth it because they're passionate about the businesses they're running.

TRUTH

2

The right business for you

Business magazines and Web sites regularly publish lists of the best businesses to start. These businesses are usually in rapidly growing industries like health care, senior services, green energy, and specialty stores. The idea is that businesses in these industries satisfy emerging environmental trends and sell products and services that are likely to be in high demand for some time. So if you started a business, would you be foolish *not* to pick a business from one of these lists?

The answer is that it depends. It depends on whether the business is something that you're passionate about and helps you meet your personal goals and aspirations. The business you select should also be congruent with your skills, abilities, aptitudes, and talents. There's a theory in organizational behavior referred to as *person-organization fit*, which says that a person's satisfaction on the job is not a function of the person or the organization but a function of the fit between the two.[1] In a start-up context, this theory is a reminder of how important it is for prospective business owners to have an accurate understanding of their abilities and skills before settling on a specific business opportunity. It's not a given that we automatically know what our best skills and aptitudes are. If you're uncertain, ask friends, family members, and coworkers for their input or seek help from a local college or university. The placement centers at public colleges and universities normally have skills assessment tests available that can help you better understand the type of business opportunity that is the best match for you.

> The best business to start is the one that matches who you are, what you know how to do, what you like to do, and what resources you have.

It's also important to have an intuitive sense of whether a particular opportunity is right for you. Tim Berry, the founder of Palo Alto Software, says that he is frequently asked by prospective business owners "What's the best business to start?" He tells people to look in the mirror. The best business to start is the one that matches who

6

you are, what you know how to do, what you like to do, and what resources you have. Berry is quick to add that a good business also has to sell a product or service that people want to buy.[2] This is a topic you'll explore more in Part II, "The Truth About Generating and Testing Business Ideas."

The business you select should also be consistent with your lifestyle expectations. The old adage "Be careful what you wish for" is as true in business as it is in other areas of life. For example, if you identify a business opportunity that has a large upside potential and obtain funding from a professional investor, you should know what to expect. Most professional investors shoot for a 30- to 40-percent annual return on their investment.[3] This level of expectation will force you into a fast growth mode literally from the start, which typically implies a quick pace of activity, a rapidly raising overhead, and a total commitment in terms of time and attention on your part. The upside is that if the new company is successful, you'll normally do well financially. If what you're really after, however, are nonfinancial rewards, such as the ability to work in an area that is personally rewarding to you or the ability to better juggle family and job-related responsibilities, you may not want the pressures associated with investors continually looking over your shoulder. A less ambitious, but perhaps more personally satisfying, business may be a better choice for you.

> The business you select should also be consistent with your lifestyle expectations. The old adage "Be careful what you wish for" is as true in business as it is in other areas of life.

TRUTH

3

Questions to ask before you quit your job

You've pretty much decided. You've picked a business idea that's a good fit for you, and you're ready to move forward. But you're nervous about quitting your job. You're just not sure when you should quit your job to start your business.

Good! Your sense of unease about quitting your job is a good thing. Making the leap from being an employee to being a business owner is a big step. You should be sure that you have identified a sound business idea and that you're fully prepared before you leave your job. There is no set formula for knowing when the timing is right to leave. But here are some questions to ask yourself as your think through your decision.

> Making the leap from being an employee to being a business owner is a big step. You should be sure that you have identified a sound business idea and that you're fully prepared before you leave your job.

- **What's the real reason you want to quit your job to start a business?** If you're quitting for a positive reason, such as passion for a business idea, you'll have a better chance of succeeding than if the reason is negative, such as you're sick of your boss or you fear you might lose your job.[1] Make sure that after your job is gone and you're working on your business, it's something you really want to do.

- **Do you have a viable business idea?** It's not good enough to simply "think" you have a viable business idea. You need to write a business plan, share it with people who can give you informed feedback, and talk to prospective customers. Don't launch a venture that's hastily conceived. Know what you're doing.

- **Are your finances in order?** You need to know your start-up costs and have sufficient cash on hand or a plan for raising the cash before you launch your business. You should also have sufficient money in the bank (experts recommend up to six months) to cover living expenses while your business gets going. What if you encounter unexpected costs? Are you willing to cut back on expenses or ask your spouse to take on an extra job to make things work?

■ **Are you emotionally ready?** Owning and running a business is different from being an employee. You'll have your own money at stake and will normally work longer hours than you did before. It's also harder to simply "leave your work behind" at the end of a day. One thing that surprises many new business owners is that they miss the hectic pace and busyness of the work environment they left, where they had frequent interactions with coworkers and others. Many new business owners work alone, especially if they work out of their homes. This type of lifestyle can be lonely and hard to get used to, particularly if you enjoy frequent interactions with others. The best way to determine what your life will be like is to get to know one or more business owners in the field you'll be entering.

■ **Can you start the business part time?** Many business owners start their businesses part time. While this approach isn't possible in all situations, you should give it some thought. By starting a business part time, you can gain valuable experience, tuck away the money you earn, and find out if you really like the business before you quit your job. In some businesses, it takes time to build a productive client list. You may be able to time the departure from your job with the point-in-time where your client list is large enough and profitable enough to justify your full-time attention.

> Have lengthy discussions with your spouse before you quit your job. Talk about both the hardships and the rewards that starting your business will entail.

■ **Is your spouse supportive?** You know from your life experiences that career-related decisions don't impact just you. If you have a spouse and kids, they'll feel the impact, too. Have lengthy discussions with your spouse before you quit your job. Talk about both the hardships and the rewards that starting your business will entail. Don't make the leap without the most important people in your life on board.

11

TRUTH

4

Key characteristics of successful business owners

Although there's no tried-and-true formula for determining who's best equipped to become a successful business owner, studies have shown that successful business owners share a set of common personal characteristics. Knowing these characteristics helps prospective business owners assess whether business ownership is a good choice for them and whether steps need to be taken to bolster their capabilities in certain areas.

Passion for their business

Passion is the enthusiasm, joy, and zeal that emerge when business owners are doing something that they feel is important and truly enjoy.[1] As mentioned in Truth 1, "Why people start businesses," passion is often the reason that people start a business. Passion is needed to infuse a business with excitement and drive and helps the founder or founders persevere through the ups and down of the startup process. It's also a source of motivation and a reward. The payoff that many business owners receive from their passion and hard work is the extreme satisfaction they experience as they work in their business and watch customers benefit from the products and services they sell. Only you can determine if you're truly passionate about a particular business idea. Many business experts say, "Don't start a business you're not passionate about." It's good advice.

> Passion is the enthusiasm, joy, and zeal that emerge when business owners are doing something that they feel is important and truly enjoy.

Tolerance for ambiguity

Tolerance for ambiguity is the ability to deal with ambiguous situations in a sensible and calm way.[2] It's context-dependent—meaning that the same situation may be ambiguous in one setting and not in another. For example, the manager of an Olive Garden restaurant may know exactly what to do if someone calls and asks if the restaurant can set aside enough tables for a group of 30 people at

7:00 p.m. that evening. The owner-manager of a new restaurant may have never had that request before and may have to stop and think about what to do. The manager might think, "I'd love to seat 30 people at the same time, but what will the people who have already waited 30 minutes for a table think if a large group walks in and is seated right away?" These types of dilemmas face the owners

Business owners with a high tolerance for ambiguity can normally handle new and uncertain situations with relative ease.

of new businesses frequently because the businesses are new and are still establishing their policies and procedures. Business owners with a high tolerance for ambiguity can normally handle new and uncertain situations with relative ease, while business owners with a low tolerance for ambiguity would handle the same situations with more angst and unease.

Self-efficacy

A critical yet not often explained characteristic of successful business owners is self-efficacy. Self-efficacy is similar to self-confidence and refers to a person's belief in being capable of performing a particular task.[3] Individuals generally avoid tasks where their self-efficacy is low and are drawn to tasks where their self-efficacy is high. As a result, a person with high self-efficacy for a given task, like starting a business, will usually approach it with enthusiasm and drive.[4] This is why some people, even though they often think about starting a business, never do it. Deep down inside, they don't believe they have the skills and abilities necessary to start and run a successful business. You can heighten your self-efficacy for starting a business by working in a field closely related to the business you're thinking about starting, becoming acquainted with people who have started successful businesses (and realizing that they are no smarter or more capable than you are), and being encouraged by others.

TRUTH

You may not need "prior business experience"

If you ask 100 people with traditional jobs why they've never started their own business, a common response that you'd get would be a lack of business experience. Most people see prior business experience as a necessary prerequisite to starting a business of their own.

In some cases, this sentiment is correct. Some businesses do take a substantial amount of experience to successfully start and run. Most financial services and medical products companies, for example, are started by people with deep industry backgrounds and business expertise. There are also technical aspects of running a business, such as finance and accounting, which take time and effort to learn and perfect, regardless of the type of business. In these instances, people who have business experience have a leg up on those who don't. It's also easy to envision the advantage that someone who has managed people and run a successful business before might have over someone who hasn't.

But there are many examples of people who've started successful businesses without prior business experience. Bill Gates of Microsoft and Michael Dell of Dell are two examples. Many people become passionate about a business idea and pursue the idea regardless of their level of prior business experiences. There are a variety of ways that people compensate for their lack of experience. Some start their business part-time and learn as they go. Others take on a partner who has business experience or make key hires early on. Still others take classes through their local Small Business Development Center or rely on SCORE (Service Core of Retired Executives) advisors for help (free, online at www.score.org).

There are also alternatives for starting a business that minimize the need for prior business experience. These alternatives allow people to pursue an opportunity in which the fundamentals of the business have already been thought out. The alternatives include franchising, direct sales,

There are many examples of people who've started successful businesses without prior business experience.

and businesses that have well-established business models.

Franchising is a form of business ownership in which a firm that already has a successful product or service (*franchisor*) licenses its trademark and method of doing business to other businesses (franchisees) in exchange for an initial franchise fee and an ongoing royalty. In some industries, such as restaurants, hotels, and automobile service, franchising is the dominant form of business ownership. Franchising provides an individual the opportunity to own a business using a tested and refined business system. The franchisor also typically provides training, technical expertise, and other forms

There are also alternatives for starting a business that minimize the need for prior business experience. These include franchising, direct sales, and businesses that have well-established business models.

of ongoing support. Many franchise systems are open to people with general skills but no prior "domain-specific" or other business experience. In fact, some franchise systems shy away from people with prior experience in the field the franchise operates in, fearing that they could have too many preconceived notions about how to run the business.

Direct sales is another option. While most people cringe when they hear the words "direct sales" (or multilevel marketing), there are legitimate direct sales opportunities. Currently, there are over 14 million people in the United States involved in direct sales.[1] Well-known direct sales companies include Tupperware, The Pampered Chef, Avon, and Discovery Toys. Although the direct sales industry as a whole suffers because of the high-pressure sales tactics of some of its members, there are an increasing number of highly legitimate opportunities. (More about this in Truth 13, "Believe it or not—There are legitimate opportunities in direct sales.") The majority of direct sales organizations do not require their participants to have prior business experience.

A third option is to start a business in an area where the business's business model is well documented and well understood. A firm's business model describes how it operates and makes money. An example of a business with a well-established business model is a bed & breakfast. Dozens of books are available that provide advice about how to open and run a successful bed & breakfast and provide instruction for how to manage day-to-day operations. Workshops are also held periodically across the country about how to open and operate a successful bed & breakfast. There are many similar examples. Following a well-established business model negates, at least in part, the prior business experience needed to launch and run one of these businesses.

TRUTH 6

The most common sources
of new business ideas

In my experience, promising new business ideas emerge from three sources: changing environmental trends, unsolved problems, and gaps in the marketplace. Select an idea that fits one of these sources. Even though you may be passionate about a particular idea or it may be a perfect fit with your skills, it still has to be an idea that people need and are willing to buy.

Changing environmental trends

The first source of business ideas is changing environmental trends. The most essential trends are economic trends, social trends, technological advances, and political action and regulatory changes. Changes in these areas often provide the impetus for new business ideas. For example, an important economic trend is the buying power of baby boomers. As baby boomers reach retirement age, a sizable portion of their spending will be redirected to areas that facilitate their retirement. This trend will invariably spawn new businesses in many areas, largely because baby boomers have greater disposable income relative to previous generations. The most promising areas include finance, travel, housing, recreation, and health care. Social trends are equally critical. Current examples include an increased focus on health and fitness, an emphasis on alternative forms of energy, and the increasing diversity of the workforce. One new company, Greasecar Fuel Systems, makes conversion kits that allow diesel engines to run on vegetable oil. The company is growing largely because its business idea is directly tied to an increased social awareness of the need to find alternatives to fossil fuels.[1]

Technological advances and political and legal changes provide ongoing sources for new business ideas. After a technology is created, products often emerge to advance it. For example, the Apple

> Even though you may be passionate about a particular idea or it may be an ideal fit with your interests and skills, it still has to be an idea that people need and are willing to buy.

iPod has created an entire industry that produces iPod accessories. It's now estimated that for every $3 spent on an iPod, at least $1 is spent on an accessory.[2] Similarly, political and legal changes often provide an opening for new business ideas. An example is the No Child Left Behind Act of 2002. The act requires states to develop assessments in basic skills to be given to all students in certain grades. Shortly after the act was passed, Kim and Jay Kleeman, two high school teachers, started Shakespeare Squared, a company that produces materials that help schools comply with the act.

Unsolved problems

The second approach to identifying business ideas is to recognize problems and find ways to solve them. Problems can be experienced or recognized by people through their jobs, hobbies, or everyday activities. For example, in 1991, Jay Sorensen dropped a cup of coffee in his lap because the paper cup was too hot. This experience led Sorensen to invent an insulating cup sleeve and to start a company to sell it. Since launching his venture, the company, Java Jacket, has sold over 1 billion cup sleeves.

Advances in technology often result in problems for people who can't use the technology in the way it's sold to the masses. For example, some older people find traditional cell phones hard to use—the buttons are small, the text is hard to read, and it's often hard to hear someone on a cell phone in a noisy room. To solve this problem, GreatCall is producing a cell phone called the Jitterbug, which is designed specifically for older users. The Jitterbug features large buttons, easy-to-read text, and a cushion that cups around the ear to improve sound quality. Another company, Firefly Mobile, is now selling a cell phone designed specifically for tweens, ages 8 to 12. The phone weighs only two ounces and is designed to fit into a kid's hand. It includes appropriate limitations for a young child and speed-dial keys for Mom and Dad.

Gaps in the marketplace

The third source of business ideas is gaps in the marketplace. There are many examples of products that consumers need or want that aren't available in a particular location or aren't available at all.

There are many examples of products that consumers need or want that aren't available in a particular location or aren't available at all.

Part of the problem is created by large retailers, like Wal-Mart and Costco, which compete primarily on price and offer the most popular items targeted toward mainstream consumers. While this approach allows the retailers to achieve economies of scale, it leaves gaps in the marketplace. This is the reason that clothing boutiques and specialty shops exist. These businesses are willing to carry merchandise that doesn't sell in large enough quantity for Wal-Mart or the other big-box retailers to sell.

There are also product gaps in the marketplace, many of which represent potentially viable business opportunities. For example, in 1997, Julie Aigner-Clark realized that there were no videos on the market to expose her one-year old daughter to music, the arts, and science, so to fill the gap she started Baby Einstein, a company that produced uplifting videos for children aged three months to three years. The company did so well it was acquired by Disney in 2001 and is still selling products under the Baby Einstein brand today.

TRUTH

7

Want several alternatives? Techniques for generating new business ideas

One thing to guard against is settling on a business idea too quickly. Whether you're just starting to look for an idea or have a notion of the business you'd like to start, it's a good idea to identify and think through several alternatives. Two common ways to generate business ideas are brainstorming and library and Internet research.

Brainstorming

Brainstorming is the process of generating several ideas about a specific topic. The approaches range from a person sitting down with a yellow legal pad and jotting down business ideas to formal "brainstorming sessions" that are led by moderators and involve a group of people. In a formal brainstorming session, the leader of the group asks the participants to share their ideas. One person shares an idea, a second person reacts to it, a third person reacts to the reaction, and so on. A flip chart or whiteboard is typically used to record the ideas. A productive brainstorming session is freewheeling and lively and is intended to generate as many substantive ideas as possible.[1]

Brainstorming sessions can also be informal. For example, during the creation of Proactiv, a popular acne treatment product, Dr. Katie Rodan, one of the company's founders, hosted dinner parties at her house and conducted brainstorming sessions with guests. Rodan credits these sessions with helping her and her cofounder develop ideas that shaped Proactiv and moved the process of starting the company along.[2] Another approach to brainstorming is to utilize the three sources for business ideas discussed in Truth 6, "The most common sources of business ideas." Imagine this. Suppose you are part of a small group that is trying to brainstorm ideas for a new type of fitness center. You create three columns on a whiteboard labeled Changing Environmental Trends, Unsolved Problems, and Gaps in the Marketplace. After brainstorming ideas in each category, a pattern jumps out at you: The population is aging, older people are increasingly interested in fitness, and many of the machines and classes taught in traditional fitness centers aren't suitable for the 50+ demographic. Based on this pattern, your first solid idea is to create a fitness center designed specifically for people 50 years old and older.

Library and Internet research

A second approach to generating business ideas is to conduct library and Internet research. A natural tendency is to think that an idea should be chosen and the process of researching the idea should then begin. The problem is that this approach is too linear. Often the best business ideas emerge when the general notion of an idea, like opening an innovative type of fitness center, is merged with extensive library and Internet research. This combination of activities is likely to provide insights into the best types of fitness centers to start.

Often the best business ideas emerge when the general notion of an idea is merged with extensive library and Internet research.

The best approach to utilizing a library is to discuss your general area of interest with a reference librarian, who can point you to useful resources, such as industry-specific magazines, trade journals, and reports. Simply browsing through several issues of a trade journal on a topic can spark new ideas. Powerful search engines and databases are also available through most university and large public libraries. An example is IBIS World, a company that publishes market research on all industries and subcategories within industries. IBIS World is a fee-based service but is normally free if accessed through a library. IBIS World has literally dozens of pages on the health and fitness club industry alone. Spending time reading this information could spark new ideas for fitness centers or help flesh out an existing idea.

Internet research is also important. If you're starting from scratch, simply type "new business ideas" into Google or Yahoo! to bring up links to newspaper and magazine articles that talk about the latest new business ideas. While these types of articles are general in nature, they provide a starting point. If you have a specific idea in mind, like the fitness center concept we've been discussing, a useful technique is to set up a Google or Yahoo e-mail alert using keywords that pertain to your topic of interest. Google and Yahoo! e-mail alerts are e-mail updates of the latest Google or Yahoo! results (that is, press releases, news articles, blog postings) based on your topic.

This technique, which is available for free, will feed you a daily stream of news articles and blog postings about specific topics.

While some people are inclined to select a business idea too quickly, other people have the opposite problem—they have trouble coming up with a sensible business idea. If this happens to you, don't get discouraged. Business ideas often take time to develop. Many people brainstorm and conduct various forms of library and Internet research for weeks or months before they settle on a specific idea.

TRUTH

A make-it or break-it issue:
Selecting an idea that can
be sold into a niche market

One rule of thumb that you should adhere to when searching for a business idea is to select an idea that you can sell into a niche market.

A niche market is a place within a larger market segment that represents a narrow group of customers with similar interests and needs. For a new business, selling into a niche market is crucial for at least two reasons. First, it allows a firm to establish itself within an industry without competing against major participants head on. Second, a niche strategy allows a firm to focus on serving a specialized market well instead of trying to be everything to everybody in a broad market, which is nearly impossible for a new entrant. An example of a firm that sells into a niche market is Prometheus Laboratories, a company that sells diagnostic services to the 15,000 doctors in the United States who specialize in gastroenterology and rheumatology. Explaining his firm's strategy of developing world-class expertise in specialized areas, then CEO Michael Walsh said, "We want to be an inch wide and a mile deep."[1]

Another way of thinking about this topic is to distinguish between vertical and horizontal markets. A vertical market, which is analogous to a niche market, focuses on similar consumers or businesses that have specific needs. For instance, a start-up business might focus on providing accounting software designed specifically for specialty eateries, like small coffee and smoothie restaurants. A horizontal market meets the needs of a broad swath of consumers or businesses, rather than a specific one. A start-up that tries to sell an accounting software product to all small businesses would be selling into a horizontal market. It's easy to imagine how much more difficult it would be for a new business to take on industry leaders and try to sell to a broad market rather than limiting itself to a smaller niche. Once a business gains momentum, it can expand into related areas and broaden the scope of its market.

> A niche market is a place within a larger market segment that represents a narrow group of customers with similar interests and needs.

Some new businesses, as a result of the nature of their industry, do compete head-to-head against larger rivals for some of their products but can still benefit by identifying niche markets to specialize in. An example is a new nursery that sells plants and lawn and garden supplies. A portion of what the nursery sells, like its

Once a business gains momentum, it can expand into related areas and broaden the scope of its market.

generic plants and its name-brand lawn and garden fertilizer, may complete against larger stores, like Home Depot and Lowe's, which often have garden centers. If this is the case, it's important that the nursery seek out niche markets, within the lawn and garden industry, which will set it apart from its larger rivals. For example, it might specialize in providing hedges, shrubbery, and sod for new construction and develop relationships with local builders and contractors. It might also become the "place to go" to purchase outdoor and indoor fountains. Specializing in these areas allows the new nursery to establish a unique identity and offsets, at least in part, the disadvantage of competing head-to-head against larger rivals on some of its products.

TRUTH

9

Screening and testing
business ideas

After you choose a business idea, test the idea to gain a sense of its feasibility. Some business owners pick an idea and immediately move forward, but it is much better to pause and spend some time scrutinizing the idea.

The proper sequence in thinking through the merits of a business idea and launching a business is as follows:

- Identifying a business idea
- Screening and testing the idea to determine its initial feasibility
- Writing a business plan
- Launching the business

Complete this process to avoid falling into the "everything about my idea is wonderful" trap.[1] All business ideas have strong and weak points, and you should be aware of both before you proceed. In addition, studies have shown that prospective business owners tend to overestimate their chances for success.[2] As a result, you need to gain an objective assessment of its potential. There are four areas to consider in testing the initial feasibility of a business idea.

Product/service feasibility—Determine if the proposed product or service is desirable and serves a need in the marketplace. Prepare a concept statement, a one-page document that includes the following:

- A description of the product or service and its benefits
- The intended target market
- A description of how the product or service will be sold
- A brief description of the company's initial management team

After you develop the statement, you should show it to 10 to 15 people who can provide informed feedback. Attach a short survey to the statement that asks the participants to (1) tell you the things they like about the product or service idea, (2) provide suggestions for making it better, (3) tell you whether they think the product or service idea is feasible, and (4) share additional comments or suggestions. Tally, read, and evaluate all responses.

Instead of developing a formal concept statement, some prospective business owners simply talk through their idea with people and gather informal feedback. Either approach is valid as long as the feedback you obtain gives you a good sense of the feasibility and desirability of your product or service idea and any areas in which it might need to be tweaked or strengthened.

Industry/niche market feasibility—The second area to explore is the industry your business will be part of and the niche market you plan to go after. The most attractive industries for new businesses have the following characteristics:

- Are large and growing rather than small and shrinking
- Are early rather than late in their life cycles
- Are important to their customers (by selling products or services that people "must have" rather than "would like to have")
- Feature environmental trends moving in favor of the industry
- Have high rather than low operating margins

You should also assess the attractiveness of the specific niche market you plan to target. An ideal market for a start-up is one that's large enough for the proposed business but small enough to avoid attracting larger competitors.

Finding good information on your industry and niche market takes a little work. The best place to start is to tap into the resources available at a university or large public library. Industry trade journals and magazines also provide information. Talking to business owners who are part of the industry you plan to enter is another option.

Organizational feasibility—The third area to explore is whether the proposed business has sufficient managerial know-how and expertise to be launched and successfully managed. This task requires the people starting the business to be honest and candid in their self-assessments. The two most important factors are the passion that the individuals have for the business and the extent to which the people involved understand the industry in which the business will compete.

There are other people-related factors that have been linked with startup success:

- Relevant industry experience or prior business start-up experience
- Depth of professional and social networks

- Experience and expertise in cash flow management
- Access to mentors or people who can provide startup advice
- Level of creativity
- Undergraduate or graduate degree

While you don't have to score high on each of these factors to be a successful business owner, looking over this list, combined with how passionate you are about the business and how well you understand the industry in which the business will compete, should give you a general sense of how prepared you are to start the proposed business.

Financial feasibility—The fourth area to consider is the financial feasibility of the proposed business. The two most central areas to consider are the total startup cash needed and the financial performance of similar businesses.

You need to have a sense of how much it will cost to launch the proposed business. Prepare a preliminary budget that lists the operating expenses and capital purchases required to get the business up and running. After you arrive at a total figure, provide an explanation of where the money will come from. If you expect the money to come from a bank loan, from an investor, or from friends and family, step back and consider how realistic those options are.

It's also good to get a sense of a proposed business's financial potential by comparing it to similar, established businesses. Again, you'll have to do some work to find the information you need. If you identify a business that is similar to the one you want to start, and the business isn't likely to be a direct competitor, it's not inappropriate to contact the owner or manager and ask about the business's sales and income. Even if the owner is only willing to talk in general terms ("our annual sales are in the $2 million range, and we're netting between $150,000 and $200,000 per year"), that information is better than nothing. Internet searches are also helpful. If you're interested in starting a fitness center, for example, typing "fitness center sales and earnings" into the Google search bar results in links to articles about fitness centers that discuss sales and earnings data.

TRUTH

10

Writing a business plan: Still as important as ever

Imagine the following. Two friends of yours are thinking about opening a seafood restaurant. After doing some preliminary analysis, they decide to write a business plan. They spend the next two months meeting five nights a week to hash out every detail of the business. They study the restaurant industry intently, identify their target market, develop a marketing plan, settle on a hiring schedule, plan their facility, determine what their startup expenses will be, and put together three years of pro forma (projected) financial statements. After 40 meetings and several drafts, they produce a 30-page business plan that explains every aspect of the business. They ask you to proofread it, and as you read through the plan, you learn about current trends in the restaurant industry, how your friends' business will take advantage of the trends, what the business will look like, how it will differentiate itself from its competitors, how much it will cost to get started, and much more.

Impressed? You have reason to be. There is convincing evidence that writing a business plan contributes to start-up success.[1] It forces the founders of a business to systematically think through every aspect of their business and develop a concrete blueprint to follow. It also creates a mechanism for a business to present itself to outsiders.[2] Most bankers and investors, for example, ask for a business plan when they are approached for funding. If you don't have a business plan, or you have to scramble to put one together, it makes a poor impression. Planning

> There is convincing evidence that writing a business plan contributes to start-up success.

also reduces anxiety and stress. Business owners who become overwhelmed during the start-up process rarely have a business plan in place. Starting a business can be a difficult and complicated process. A well-written business plan normally anticipates and provides solutions for handling the hardest and trickiest issues.[3]

Most business plans are 20 to 35 pages and are divided into sections that represent the major aspects of a new venture's business.

A sample plan is as follows:

I. Executive Summary

II. Company Description

III. Industry Analysis

IV. Market Analysis

V. Marketing Plan

VI. Management Team and Company Structure

VII. Operations Plan

VIII. Product (or Service) Design and Development Plan

IX. Financial Projections

Appendixes

The title of the sections varies from plan to plan, as does the quality of the writing, the substance of the plan, and the degree to which the plan convinces the reader that the business opportunity is exciting, feasible, and within the capabilities of the people launching the business. Writing a business plan that includes all these elements is not an easy task, but it is a fulfilling and useful one. Think back to the vignette that opened this chapter. Although the two individuals sacrificed 40 evenings to write their plan, just think how much they learned through the process and how much more confident and self-assured they'll be when they launch their business. They'll also have a blueprint to follow and will have a plan available to provide to bankers or investors if needed.

Publications on how to write a business plan are available at bookstores, and Small Business Development Centers and SCORE chapters often sponsor workshops on how to write a business plan. [4] Some businesses hire consultants or outside advisors to write their business plans. Although there's nothing wrong with getting advice and making sure a plan looks as professional as possible, an outside

> One possible outcome of writing a business plan is that it may show that a particular business isn't feasible.

person shouldn't be the author of the plan. Besides listing facts and figures, a business plan needs to project a sense of anticipation and excitement about the possibilities surrounding a new venture, which is a task best accomplished by the creators of the business. Plus, hiring someone to write the plan denies the prospective business owners the positive benefits of the writing experience.

One possible outcome of writing a business plan is that it may show that a particular business isn't feasible. While reaching that conclusion may be regrettable, it is better to fail on paper than in real life.

TRUTH

11

Starting from scratch: Developing your own product or service

There are four common ways to get into business: starting from scratch, buying a franchise, participating in direct sales, and buying an existing business. When most people think of starting a business, they think of starting from scratch. This approach involves developing your own business idea and building the business from the ground up. But there are pluses and minuses to each method of getting into business. This Truth focuses on the advantages and disadvantages of starting a business from scratch.

Advantages of starting a business from scratch

Starting a business from scratch is the ultimate business start-up experience. You start with a clean slate and are able to shape and mold the business as you see fit. You select (or develop) the product or service you will sell, pick the business's name, select a location, and build the business. If you're careful, you can often start and build the business fairly inexpensively. In fact, the average business in the United States is started for about $10,000.[1] Even aggressive growth firms, in most cases, don't take an arm and leg to start. Every year *Inc.* magazine compiles a list of the 500 fastest-growing privately owned businesses in the United States. In 2006, the medium amount it took to start one of the businesses on the list was $75,000.[2] That means that half of them were started for less than $75,000. It's normally more expensive to buy a franchise or purchase an existing business.

> Starting a business from scratch is the ultimate business start-up experience.

Starting a business from scratch, for many people, is also very satisfying. The business is a direct reflection of your efforts, values, work ethic, and skills. It's also the most practical way for a prospective business owner to bring a new product or service idea to market. While there are many advantages to franchising, participating in direct sales, and buying an existing business (as discussed in Truths 12 to 14), these approaches require you to build on someone else's product or service idea. Additionally, if you're starting a business to fill an aspiration gap, such as being home by 3:00 p.m.

on workdays to meet the school bus or having Sundays free to participate in volunteer activities, starting a business from scratch may be your best alternative. Many people who buy retail franchises, for example, find the hours of operation and other rules to be so rigid that they have to plan their lives around their business. While starting a business from scratch is in many ways more demanding than other ways of getting into business, the owner has the advantage of setting the hours of operation and the overall tone for the business.

Disadvantages of starting a business from scratch

There are also disadvantages to starting a business from scratch. Starting a new business entails greater risk than buying a franchise, participating in a direct sales organization, or buying an existing business. You must also build your business's brand, develop a marketing campaign, establish relationships with suppliers, and complete the other chores necessary to build a business from its inception. While many people enjoy engaging in these activities, they are time-consuming and require expertise. As mentioned in Truth 5, "You may not need prior business experience," one of the principle advantages of franchising and direct sales, in particular, is that the fundamentals of the business have already been worked out.

It's also more difficult to obtain financing for a new business than it is to buy a franchise or purchase an existing business. There is always a certain degree of skepticism surrounding a brand-new business. The skepticism can be lessened through a well-developed business plan, as discussed in Truth 10, "Writing a business plan: Still as important as ever." A new business doesn't have a track record to rely on. One of the primary advantages of buying a franchise, such as a Subway or a Curves International, is that the business concept is proven, which is reassuring to bankers and investors. The same rationale applies to buying an existing business. As a result of these realities, the same person who is unable to secure a $50,000 loan to start a business from scratch may be able to borrow two to three times that amount to buy a franchise or an existing business. The perceived risk involved with starting a business from scratch is that much higher than the other alternatives.

Making the call—Is starting a business from scratch the right strategy for you?

In general, individuals who have prior business experience are best-suited to start a business from scratch. It also helps to have access to start-up funds through personal savings or via loans from friends and family. These are not hard-and-fast rules, however. Many people have started successful businesses from scratch with no prior business experience and limited start-up funds. The best strategy for making the call is to weigh the advantages and disadvantages of starting a business from scratch against the alternatives for your own circumstances.

> In general, individuals who have prior business experience are best-suited to start a business from scratch.

TRUTH

12

Franchising:
Buying into someone
else's formula for success

Franchising is a form of business ownership in which a firm that already has a successful product or service (franchisor) licenses its trademark and method of doing business to other businesses (franchisees) in exchange for an initial franchise fee and ongoing royalties. The total initial investment includes the franchise fee, the costs associated with getting the franchise up and running (which vary by franchise), and any other fees that are part of the franchise agreement. The ongoing royalty fee, which is usually around 6 percent, is based on a percentage of weekly or monthly gross income.

Advantages of buying a franchise

There are two primary advantages to buying a franchise as opposed to starting a business from scratch. First, franchising provides a small business owner the opportunity to own a business using a tested and refined business system. This attribute reduces the time and the amount of experience needed to get a franchise business going. In addition, the trademark that comes with the franchise provides instant legitimacy for the business. For instance, if you're interested in opening a fitness center for women, you'll likely attract more customers by opening a Curves or Lady of America franchise than a new, independently owned business. The second advantage to buying a franchise is that the franchisor typically provides training, technical expertise, and other forms of ongoing support. For example, if you buy a Curves franchise, your initial investment gets you a weeklong training program at Club Camp—which is Curve's training center in Waco, Texas. Additional training is provided at regional events and at the company's annual meeting, and any franchisee needing a refresher can return to Club Camp for free. This type of support is what attracts people of all backgrounds to the franchise concept, regardless of their prior work experiences. "We get people from all walks of life, says Cassie Findley, director of continuing education

> Franchising provides a small business owner the opportunity to own a business using a tested and refined business system.

and research at Curves. "We get homemakers who want to become entrepreneurs and run their own businesses. We get retirees who want to help women change their lives, and we get a small percentage of investors. They're not physical fitness professionals when they come to us."[1]

Disadvantages of buying a franchise

The main disadvantages of buying a franchise are the costs involved and the loss of some of your independence as a business owner. The total initial investment to get a franchise up and running varies from $31,400 to $53,500 for a Curves franchise (depending on the location and other factors) to $74,900 to $222,800 for a Subway. The monthly royalty payments are permanent. While there are similar costs involved with starting a business from scratch, there are no ongoing royalty payments. In regard to independence, many franchise systems are sticklers about doing things in a specific manner. McDonald's and other fast-food retailers, for example, are strict in terms of their restaurants' appearance and how their food is prepared. As a result, franchising is typically not a good fit for people who like to experiment with their own ideas and are independent.

Ultimately, franchising represents an attractive middle ground for many people. So says Joe Cummings, the purchaser of a PostNet franchise. A PostNet franchise is similar to a FedEx Kinko's store. After a 21-year career with Bristol-Myers, Cummings took a buyout and spent a year deciding on what to do next. Commenting on why he settled on a PostNet franchise rather than opening his own business, Cummings said, "I wanted to get what I call the best of both worlds—the support of a proven system in an environment that's really entrepreneurial. I felt a franchise was the best way to do that."[2]

> The main disadvantages of buying a franchise are the costs involved and the loss of some of your independence as a business owner.

Caution

One note of caution: You should be careful if you decide to buy into a franchise system. While there are many excellent franchise systems to choose from, some systems never live up to the level of support promised. The best way to check out the merits of a franchisor is to ask for the names, addresses, and phone numbers of several of the franchisor's current franchisees and then call these individuals and ask them about their experiences. You can also ask for a copy of the franchisor's Franchise Disclosure Document (FDD), which contains detailed information about the background and financial health of the franchisor.

TRUTH

13

Believe it or not:
There are legitimate
opportunities in direct sales

While most people wince or cringe when they hear the words "direct sales" (or "multilevel marketing"), there are attractive and legitimate direct sales opportunities. The industry is dominated by women (85.2 percent), who normally enter direct sales part-time as a way of earning extra income.[1] There are over 15.2 million people in the United States involved in direct sales, and the number keeps growing.[2] Well-known companies include Tupperware, The Pampered Chef, Creative Memories, and Mary Kay. Many direct sales organizations are large and growing. The Pampered Chef alone has over 60,000 independent sales consultants. Its consultants conduct over one million in-home demonstrations, called Cooking Shows, every year.[3]

Many people have negative feelings toward the direct sales industry because they have either personally been subjected to a high-pressure sales pitch or know someone who has. Although the industry as a whole suffers as a result of these types of sales tactics, not all direct sales firms fit this stereotype. The Pampered Chef is an example of a direct sales organization that exemplifies the good in the industry. Started by Doris Christopher in 1980, the integrity and stature of the company is such that it was acquired by Berkshire Hathaway in 2002. Berkshire Hathaway is controlled by Warren Buffett, one of the most respected and well-known investors in the world. In the Foreword to the book, *The Pampered Chef*, in which Christopher chronicles the history of the company, Buffett writes,

> "*The Pampered Chef is truly loved by its customers because it has found a need and filled it exceptionally well, helping everyday home cooks to become masters of their own home kitchens and making mealtime preparations quick, easy, and fun. It also offers its consultants an incomparable business opportunity, allowing men and women to build a home-based business of their own, based on Doris Christopher's*

personal blueprint for success. When you read the profiles of The Pampered Chef's Kitchen Consultants in Chapter 8, you may wonder what you're doing in your nine-to-five cubicle while these folks are happy cooking their way to fame and fortune."[4]

Most people start with an organization like The Pampered Chef part-time and only make it a full-time job if they do extremely well. The sales typically take place through in-home sales demonstrations or parties, although an increasing percentage of direct sales are taking place online. In addition to selling the product, you recruit others to sell the product for you. You then receive a percentage of your recruits' sales. This facet of direct sales is one of its biggest lures. It allows you to earn income from your efforts along with the efforts of the people you recruit. It also incents the person who signed you up to provide you ongoing mentoring and support, since that person also receives a percentage of your sales.

If you go the direct sales route, make sure you pick a company that sells a product or service that you're passionate about. Since the majority of your sales will come through one-on-one product demonstrations or home parties, you'll need to convey a genuine interest and passion for the product you're selling to be successful. The biggest mistake that people make when they go into direct sales is to become more enamored with the "financial opportunity" than the product or service they sell.

> The biggest mistake that people make when they go into direct sales is to become more enamored with the "financial opportunity" rather than the product or service that they sell.

You should also be careful about the specific direct sales organization that you sign up with. Avoid organizations that require you to buy a ton of product upfront or promise that you'll get rich with little effort. One way to minimize the chances that you'll select a company you'll later regret is to restrict your selection to organizations that are members of the Direct Selling

Association (www.dsa.org), a highly respected industry trade group. To become a member of the Direct Selling Association, a firm has to go through a rigorous one-year application process and abide by the organization's Code of Ethics. Currently, only 213 of more than 1,000 direct sales organizations that exist are members. If an organization is not a member of the Direct Sales Association, and you're still interested in joining, you should, at a minimum, check the company's history with your local Better Business Bureau, your state's Attorney General, and the Federal Trade Commission.

TRUTH

14

Buying a business

If you're intrigued by the idea of owning and operating a business but don't want to start a business from scratch or pursue franchising or direct sales, a final option is to buy an existing business. Although there are many rewards associated with building a business from the ground up, there are distinct advantages to buying a business that's already established. There will also be an increasing number of businesses for sale to choose from. An estimated 65 percent to 75 percent of all small businesses in the United States—some 10 million—will likely go up for sale over the next five to ten years as a result of the retirement of baby boomers.[1]

There are two primary advantages to buying an existing business. First, you avoid the time and expense involved with selecting and testing a business idea. Second, you start, on day one, with a business that has customers and an established cash flow.[2] You'll also have an easier time obtaining financing or funding. Bankers like to see three to five years of proven performance before they lend money to a business. As mentioned in Truth 11, "Starting from scratch: Developing your own product or service," this reality works to the advantage of the buyers of existing businesses and to the disadvantage of businesses started from scratch.

> Although there are many rewards associated with starting a business and building it from the ground up, there are distinct advantages to buying a business that's already established.

All told, there are ten primary advantages to buying a business versus starting one from scratch:

- Established customers

- Established products or services

- No time invested in picking and testing a business idea (at least initially—new products or services may be added later)

- Proven business concept and processes

- Trained employees

- Business generates cash flow from day one

- Established suppliers

- Easier to obtain financing or funding

- Seller may lend support and assist with financing

- Lower risk of failure

An existing business may also offer amenities, like an ideal location, which you'd never be able to replicate starting a similar business from scratch.

The primary disadvantage to buying an existing business is the cost. The hard work involved with starting and building a business, along with the customers and cash flow that come with it, is built into the purchase price. This intangible is often called *goodwill*, which is the excess of the purchase price over the value of the assets of the business. So it's generally more expensive to buy an existing business than it is to start a similar one from scratch. There is also the possibility of hidden costs. For example, some of a business's best employees may leave once the business changes hands, even if they indicated they would stay. Similarly, receivables that were thought to be collectable may turn out to be uncollectable. You can anticipate these types of complications and build them into your offer price to a degree, but it's hard to anticipate everything, and disappointments often occur.

It's also hard to find a profitable business for sale at a reasonable price. Business owners often have an inflated idea of the market value of their business. In addition, it's not uncommon for the owners of businesses with fading potential to try to unload them, regardless of how good they try to make them appear. Still, thousands of businesses are bought and sold every year with good results. The most common places to look for businesses for sale include

- Newspaper classified advertising under "Business Opportunities"

- Business opportunity magazines, which are available at major bookstores

- Business brokers (identified through yellow pages advertising and Internet searches)

- Word of mouth through friends, family, and business acquaintances

- Internet searches (listed under "business opportunities" or "businesses for sale")

Proceed cautiously and thoroughly check out the businesses that spark your interest.

Proceed cautiously and thoroughly check out the businesses that spark your interest. If you get serious about a particular business, hire an attorney to represent you. You may also want to hire an accountant to help you go over the business's books. While you'll have to swallow hard when these professionals quote their fees, it's normally small potatoes compared to making a major mistake in the process of buying a business.

TRUTH

15

Internet businesses: The sky does seem to be the limit

Although starting an Internet business isn't a distinct business-entry strategy, like starting a business from scratch or buying a franchise, many people put it in a category of its own. The Internet, as a place to do business, continues to grow, and there are a number of ways that individuals are starting part-time and full-time businesses that are strictly online.

While many Internet businesses simply sell products or services online rather than through brick-and-mortar stores, one of the beauties of the Internet is that you don't have to have a product or service to sell to support an online business. If you know a lot about a particular topic, such as cooking, investments, or home repair, you can launch a Web site, populate it with articles and other useful information, and make money by essentially selling access to the people you attract to your Web site. You do this by selling advertising space on the Web site. This one factor has enabled numerous people to convert hobbies and personal interests into part-time and full-time online businesses.

People make money online in a variety of ways; however, this Truth focuses on how people support part-time and full-time businesses via Web sites. The two most common ways are e-commerce Web sites and advertising-supported special-interest Web sites.

E-commerce Web sites

E-commerce refers to the direct buying and selling of products and services online. Most e-commerce companies sell products, although there are a growing number of online businesses that sell services. People opt to sell products and services online rather than through traditional means for a variety of reasons. Some online stores are set up to sell a product that wouldn't sell in sufficient volume to support a brick-and-mortar store. An example is Oddball Shoe Company (www.oddballshoe.com), a Web that sells a size 16 EEEE athletic shoe for men and similar odd-sized shoes. Another rationale for an online store is to gain a broad audience for a specialty item. An example is Wadee (www.wadee.com), a Web site that sells handmade children's toys.

There are two ways that Web sites that sell products are set up. Some companies make their own products or stock products made by others and then ship them to customers when they receive an order. Other companies utilize a process referred to as *drop shipping*. Drop shippers feature an online storefront but don't have inventory. Instead, when they take an order, they pass

Some online stores are set up to sell a product that wouldn't sell in sufficient volume to support a brick-and-mortar store.

it on to a wholesaler or manufacturer, who fills the order and then ships it directly to the customer—usually in a box with the online retailer's name and invoice inside. By utilizing this method, an online merchant earns a lower margin than it would if it controlled the entire process itself, but its costs are lower, too. It also doesn't get stuck with inventory that goes out of style. eBags (www.ebags.com), an e-commerce company that sells luggage, backpacks, and similar items, is an example of a drop shipper.

Advertising-supported special interest Web sites

The second type of Web site that supports part-time or full-time businesses is an advertising-supported special interest Web site. These sites post articles, tips, and other forms of information about a specific topic or category of topics and make money by attracting visitors to the site and then selling advertising to companies interested in reaching those visitors. There are three ways to sell advertising on a Web site:

■ **Pay-per-click programs**—A pay-per-click program places ads on Web sites, and the owner of the site is paid a small commission every time someone clicks on the ad. All the major search engines sponsor pay-per-click ad programs. Examples include Google's AdSense, Yahoo! Search Marketing, and MSN adCenter. The most compelling aspect of pay-per-click programs is that they deliver contextually relevant ads. This means the ads mirror the content of your site, which is good for the advertiser and helps boost your commissions.

A pay-per-click program places ads on Web sites, and the owner of the site is paid a small commission every time someone clicks on the ad.

- **Affiliate programs**—An affiliate program is a way for online merchants, like 1-800-FLOWERS or Amazon.com, to get more exposure by offering a commission to Web sites that are willing to feature ads for their products or services. In most cases, the ads are small text ads, and the merchant sponsoring the program pays the affiliate a small commission every time someone clicks on the ad and buys one of its products or services.

- **Direct ads**—You can also go directly to advertisers and sell space on your Web site. These ads tend to be banner ads, *skyscraper ads* (tall ads that run along the side of a Web site), or ads with pictures that are embedded in the content of a Web site. If you run ads like these on your Web site, you're paid a commission based on either the number of times an ad is clicked or the number of times it is seen (that is, the number of *impressions*).

An example of an advertising-supporting Web site that has good content and generates substantial revenue is Ask the Builder (www.askthebuilder.com), which is sponsored by Tim Carter, a well-known columnist on home repair. Information and instructions on all types of home building projects and repair are available on this Web site, as are links to areas that focus on specific topics, like air conditioning, deck construction, and plumbing. Clicking any one of these areas brings up Google AdSense ads that deal with that specific area. All together, the site has hundreds of AdSense ads. Carter can do this and still attract large numbers of visitors because the information he provides is good and helpful.

TRUTH

16

Choosing a location for your business

As a new business prepares to get up and running, there are a number of decisions that must be made. One of the most significant is where the business will be located. A good choice of location can help a business get off to a solid start, while a poor choice can have the opposite effect. A poor choice can also be difficult to fix, particularly if a business signs a long-term lease or purchases property.

Fortunately, there is a standard set of issues to consider when selecting a business's location.

For some businesses, location is key, while for others it's almost irrelevant. For example, many service businesses—such as painters, electricians, mail-order companies, and Internet businesses—don't interface directly with the public, so their physical location isn't a major issue. In fact, these businesses often seek out nondescript locations to economize on costs. In contrast, location is an extremely crucial issue for retail stores, certain service businesses, and professional practices (like doctor's offices) that deal directly with the public.

> A good choice of location can help get a business get off to a solid start, while a poor choice can have the opposite effect.

If location is important, what type of location will work best for you?

The key consideration here is to pick a location that will increase your flow of customers. Start by asking yourself the following questions:

- Will my customers come on foot, or will they drive and need a place to park?

- Will more customers come if the business is located near other similar businesses?

- Will more customers come if the business is located near complementary businesses?

- Do the demographics of the trade area the business will be located in make a difference?

Answering these four questions can go a long way in helping a business owner select an appropriate location. For example, if you're opening an urban bagel shop or a similar type of business, you'll want to locate in an area that has a high amount of foot traffic. In contrast, if you're opening an auto parts store or a convenience store, you'll want to be on a busy street where the store can be seen by drivers who can pull into your parking lot. In terms of being near similar businesses, clothing stores and jewelry stores, for example, often benefit by being near similar businesses, since people like to comparison shop. A hair salon or barber shop, where comparison shopping isn't as much of an issue, may do better by itself. Some businesses benefit by locating near a big-box store like Wal-Mart or Target, because their customer bases are similar and they benefit from the increased traffic. An example is Sally's Beauty Supply, which appears in 26 percent of U.S. Wal-Mart-anchored shopping centers.[1] Similarly, some businesses benefit by being located near complementary businesses. Ice cream shops, for example, do better when they're located near movie theaters and restaurants.

An extremely important issue is whether the demographic makeup of a trade area is suitable for a particular business. A high-end clothing boutique, for example, needs to be in an affluent area. Stores that sell children's clothing do better in areas with a high percentage of young families than in areas with a high percentage of retirement-age people. You can obtain the demographic breakdown of most communities in the United States (and even zip codes within communities) via American FactFinder (http://factfinder.census.gov), which is a Census Bureau Web site. Another good source is City-Data. com (www.cita-data.com), which contains similar and often more current demographic information on U.S. cities and towns.

How much can you afford?

A third consideration is how much you can afford. This is a tough issue, because the best locations invariably are the most expensive. Most businesses that aren't home-based businesses rent or lease property rather than build or buy, which reduces the cost some.[2] The best way to determine the rental or lease rates for a particular area is to talk to a real estate broker or agent. Ultimately, a business can only occupy premises that it can afford. There is no practical way around this issue other than to carefully weigh your financial priorities. In some cases, a business, like an urban bagel shop, may be better off spending more than originally budgeted on a premium location and less than originally budgeted on ancillary items like computer equipment or the restaurant's decor. You need to dedicate limited resources to the areas that ultimately will make the largest positive impact on your business.

Is the physical structure you're considering adequate?

Once you locate a property to lease or rent, you should be careful to make sure it is adequate for your business. For example, if you are considering space for an Internet business, it will need to be wired to connect to a fiber-optic network or a T1 line (high-volume Internet connection). If you will be cooking in a building, it may need to be vented in a certain manner and need additional plumbing and electric work. While these issues may seem obvious, it's often a matter of negotiation regarding who will pay for the upgrades that are needed. If you can't convince the landlord to do the necessary work, a seemingly ideal location may be cost-prohibitive. There are other issues that are potentially negotiable, so make sure you think through your circumstances carefully. For example, if you open a retail store in an enclosed mall or strip mall, you can often negotiate what's called a *restrictive covenant* to prevent the landlord from leasing space to one of your direct competitors.

Complying with local zoning laws is another principal issue. Never sign a lease and occupy a property until you're confident it's zoned for your type of business.

TRUTH

17

Something you'll say a million times: Your business's name

While at first glance naming a business may seem like a minor issue, it is an extremely important one. A company's name is one of the first things people associate with a business. Keep in mind that it is a word or phrase that will be said thousands or hundreds of thousands of times during the life of a business. A company's name is also the most critical aspect of its branding strategy. A business's name must facilitate rather than hinder how the business wants to differentiate itself in the marketplace and how it wants to be viewed by its customers.

> The primary consideration in naming a business is that the name should complement the type of business the company plans to be.

The primary consideration in naming a business is that the name should complement the type of business the company plans to be. It is helpful to divide companies into four categories to discuss this issue.

Consumer-driven companies

If a company plans to focus on a particular type of customer, its name should reflect the attributes of its clientele. For example, a clothing store that specializes in small sizes for women is called La Petite Femme. Similarly, an online store that sells clothing for big and tall men and boys is named Big and Tall Guys. A company that installs cameras in day care centers and allows parents to log on to a password-protected Web site to see their children during the day is called ParentWatch. These companies have names that were chosen to appeal specifically to their target market or clientele.

Product- or service-driven companies

If a company plans to focus on a particular product or service, its name should reflect the advantages that its product or service brings to the marketplace. Examples include 1-800-FLOWERS, Whole Foods Markets, XM Satellite Radio, and Jiffy Print. These names were chosen to reflect the distinctive attributes of the product or service the company offers, regardless of the clientele.

Industry-driven companies

If a company plans to focus on a broad range of product or services in a particular industry, its name should reflect the category it is participating in. Examples include Sports Authority, Bed Bath & Beyond, Toys R Us, and Home Depot. These companies have names that are intentionally broad and are not limiting in regard to target market or product selection.

Personality- or image-driven companies

Some companies are founded by individuals who put such an indelible stamp on the company that it may be smart to name the company after the founder. Examples include Charles Schwab, The Trump Organization, Calvin Klein, and Magic Johnson Enterprises. These companies have names that benefit from a positive association with a particular person or distinctive founder. Of course, this strategy can backfire if the founder falls out of favor in the public's eye.

Other considerations

There are also some general rules of thumb for naming a business. Select a name that is easy to spell, easy to pronounce, and doesn't limit the future expansion of the business. For example, a name like Sally's Sewing Supplies isn't a good choice. It's easy to spell and pronounce, but at some point the business might want to expand beyond sewing supplies. Once you settle on a name, you should contact the Secretary of State's office in the state where you're located to make sure the name is available. If it is, you should reserve it in the manner recommended by the Secretary of State. You should also trademark the name.

> Select a name that is easy to spell, easy to pronounce, and doesn't limit the future expansion of the business.

Information about how to trademark a business's name is discussed in Truth 35, "Trademarks: An essential form of protection."

A final factor to consider in selecting a name for a business is whether its Internet domain name is available. This can be a frustrating endeavor, because the majority of the most obvious names have already been taken. If the name you've chosen for your business isn't available, don't panic. A little ingenuity can go a long way. You can normally either tweak the name of your business or your Internet domain name to make things work. For example, suppose you have decided to open a restaurant that will feature low-fat dishes and have settled on the name Healthy Options. You check and find that the Internet domain name www.healthyoptions.com is taken. You don't need to give up on the Healthy Options name. You can vary the Internet domain name as long as it makes sense. For example, at the time this book was written, the Internet domain name www.healthyoptionsrestaurant.com was available—a perfectly acceptable Internet domain name for your business.

TRUTH

18

The paper chase: Obtaining business licenses and permits

If you're anxious to get your business started, the last thing you normally want to do is deal with government paperwork. Do it anyway. It's important to obtain the licenses and permits you need. You can also be subject to stiff penalties if you don't comply in a timely manner.

Most of the licenses and permits you'll need are required to be in place before your business opens. They vary by city, county, and state, as well as by the type of business you plan to start, so study the regulations carefully. Some licenses are difficult to get—such as liquor licenses. For example, in some states, the only way to get a liquor license is to buy a preexisting license. This stipulation often results in a bidding war when someone is willing to give up their liquor license, which increases the price. Enjoy the paper chase.

> Most of the licenses and permits you'll need are required to be in place before your business opens.

Obtaining a business license

Most communities require businesses to obtain a license to operate. Your city clerk should be able to handle this for you. If you plan to operate your business from home, a separate home occupation business license is often required. When you apply for a license, your city planning and zoning department will usually check to make sure your area is zoned for the purpose you want to use it for. If your business is located outside a city or town's jurisdiction, you'll need to go to your county courthouse to obtain your business license.

If you're a sole proprietor, you can usually stop here, as far as your business license goes. If you have employees, or your business is a corporation, a limited liability company, or a limited partnership, you'll need a state business license in addition to your local one. There are additional state provisions that you may need to comply with. If you're starting a retail or service business, you'll need to obtain a sales tax license, which enables you to collect taxes on the state's behalf. You'll need a special license to sell liquor, lottery tickets, gasoline, or firearms. People in certain professions, such as barbers, chiropractors, nurses, and real estate agents, must normally pass a state examination and maintain a professional license to conduct business. This category covers a wide swath of businesses, so check with your state government to see if your profession applies. Certain businesses also require special state licenses. Examples

> If you're starting a retail or service business, you'll need to obtain a sales tax license, which enables you to collect taxes on the state's behalf.

include child care, health care facilities, hotels, and restaurants. Again, check with your state to see if your business is subject to special licensing and inspection requirements.

A narrow group of businesses are required to have a federal business license, including investment advising, drug manufacturing, preparation of meat products, broadcasting, interstate trucking, and businesses that manufacture tobacco, alcohol, or firearms, or sell firearms. These licenses are obtained through the Federal Trade Commission.

Nearly all business are required to obtain a federal *employer identification number (EIN)*, also known as a tax identification number, which is used in filing various business tax returns. The only exception is sole proprietors who do not have employees. In this instance, the sole proprietor uses his social security number as the tax identification number. You can obtain a tax identification number free from the Internal Revenue Service by calling 800-829-4933.

Permits

Along with obtaining the appropriate business licenses, you may need to obtain one or more business permits, depending on your location and the nature of your business. The permits regulate how you do business. For example, if you plan to sell food, either as a restaurateur or as a wholesaler to other retailers, you'll need a city or county health department permit. If your business will be open to the public or will use flammable material, you may need a fire department permit. Some communities require businesses to obtain a permit to put up a sign. Because requirements vary from city to city on these and other issues, you'll need to ask around to see if any special permits are required for your business. If you're occupying a building, there will also be building code requirements you'll have to comply with.

All businesses that plan to use a fictitious name, which is any name other than the business owner's name, need a fictitious business name permit (also called a *dba* or *doing business as*). If you're a sole proprietor, you can obtain the permit at the city or county level. For example, if your name is Sarah Ryan and you apply for a business license, your business will be registered as Sarah Ryan. If you want to use another name, like Gulf Coast Fresh Flowers, you must apply for a fictitious name permit. You normally need a fictitious name permit to obtain a checking account in your business's name. It's also important to have a fictitious name permit if you execute any contracts, sign any agreements, or pay bills or accept payments under your business's name.

Sources of assistance

There are a number of resources available to assist business owners in identifying the proper licenses and permits to apply for. The Small Business Administration (SBA) maintains a Web site, at www.sba.gov/hotlist/license.html, that features links that provide information on how to obtain a business license in each state. In addition, most major bookstores, like Borders and Barnes & Noble, carry publications that talk about "doing business in" whatever state you are located in. These publications normally cover business licensing and permit procedures for the applicable state. Many city governments also publish documents that provide guidance for doing business in their city. Good places to look for these publications are the city government's Web site, the city library's Web site, or the Web site for the local Chamber of Commerce. For example, the Dallas Public Library publishes a publication titled "Starting a Small Business in Dallas: A Resource Guide." The guide is available via the Dallas Public Library's Web site at http://dallaslibrary.org/CGI/smallbiz.htm.

TRUTH

19

Choosing a form of business ownership

When you launch a business, you need to choose a form of legal entity. Sole proprietorship, partnerships, corporations, and limited liability companies are the most common. There is no single form of business ownership that works best in all situations.

Sole proprietorship—The simplest form of business ownership is the sole proprietorship,[1] which involves one person. The person and the business are essentially the same. The biggest advantage of the sole proprietorship is that the owner maintains complete control over the business. The biggest disadvantage is that the sole proprietor is responsible for all the liabilities of the business. If a sole proprietor's business is sued, the owner could theoretically lose all the business's assets along with personal assets. As a result, a sole proprietorship is not a good choice for most new businesses.

Advantages of a sole proprietorship:

- Creating one is easy and inexpensive.
- The owner maintains complete control of the business and profits.
- It is not subject to double taxation (explained later).

Disadvantages of a sole proprietorship:

- Liability on the owner's part is unlimited.
- The business ends at the owner's death or loss of interest in the business.
- The liquidity of the owner's investment is low.

Partnerships—If two or more people start a business, they must organize as a partnership, corporation, or limited liability company. Partnerships are organized as either general or limited partnerships. The primary advantage of a general partnership is that the business isn't dependent on a single person for its success. The primary disadvantage of a general partnership is that the individual partners are liable for all the partnership's obligations. As a result, a general partnership is typically not a good choice for a new business.

Advantages of a general partnership:

- Creating one is easy and inexpensive.
- Business losses can be deducted against the partner's other sources of income.

■ It is not subject to double taxation (explained later).

Disadvantages of a general partnership:

■ Liability on the part of each general partner is unlimited.

■ Disagreements among partners can occur.

■ The liquidity of each partner's investment is low.

The second form of partnership is the limited partnership. The primary difference between the two is that a limited partnership includes two classes of owners: general partners and limited partners. The general partners are liable for the obligations of the partnership, but the limited partners are liable only up to the amount of their investment.

Corporations—A corporation is a separate legal entity organized under the authority of a state. Corporations are organized as either C corporations or subchapter S corporations. A C corporation is a legal entity that is separate from its owners. The major advantage of a corporation is that it shields its owners from personal liability for obligations of the business. The major disadvantage is that a corporation is subject to double-taxation—the corporation is taxed on its net income and, when the same income is distributed to shareholders in the form of dividends, it is taxed again on the shareholder's personal income tax returns.

Advantages of a C corporation:

■ Owners are liable only for the obligations of the corporation up to the amount of their investment.

■ No restrictions on the number of shareholders.

■ The ability to share stock with employees through incentive plans can be a powerful form of employee motivation.

Disadvantages of a C corporation:

■ Setting up and maintaining one is more difficult and expensive than a sole proprietorship or general partnership.

■ Business losses cannot be deducted against the shareholder's other sources of income.

■ Income is subject to double taxation.

A subchapter S corporation combines the advantages of a partnership and a C corporation. It is similar to a partnership in that the profits and losses of the business are not subject to double taxation. It is similar to a corporation in that the owners are not subject to personal liability for the behavior of the business. The major disadvantage of the subchapter S corporation is that it is limited to 100 shareholders, which can be a drawback when trying to raise money from a large pool of investors.

Limited liability company—The limited liability company (LLC) is a form of business organization that is gaining popularity in the United States. The main advantages of the LLC are that it is more flexible than a subchapter S corporation in terms of number of owners and tax-related issues, and all members enjoy limited liability. The main disadvantages are that it is relatively complex to set up, and in some states the rules governing the LLC vary.

Advantages of a limited liability company:

- Members are liable for the obligations of the business only up to the amount of their investment.
- The number of shareholders is unlimited.
- There is no double taxation.

Disadvantages of a limited liability company:

- Setting up and maintaining one is more difficult and expensive than the other legal entities.
- Some of the regulations governing LLCs vary by state.
- Some states levy a franchise tax on LLCs, which is essentially a fee the LLC pays the state for the benefit of limited liability.

According to a study published by the Kauffman Foundation, 35.5% of businesses start as sole proprietorships, 30.5% start as LLCs, 20.1% start as subchapter S corporations, 7.9% start as C corporations, and 5.7% start as limited or general partnerships.[2] It is money well spent to consult with a small business accountant or attorney to select the form of business ownership most appropriate for your start-up.

TRUTH

20

Creating a Web site:
An absolute necessity

Imagine the following scenario. Your 10th wedding anniversary is coming up, and you and your spouse have talked about trying a new restaurant, called Helen's Grill, which just opened. You want to make sure the evening is special, so you decide to learn more about the restaurant. You go to Helen's Grill's Web site and view pictures of its interior, look at the menu, read comments from satisfied customers, and click on a link labeled "Reservations for special occasions." You find that the restaurant will set up a table for you and your spouse with fresh flowers, a bottle of wine, and a personalized anniversary greeting. You make the reservation. Helen's Grill acquires a new customer.

If you're starting a business, you need to be like Helen's Grill. You need a Web site to introduce yourself to customers, share information about your business, and conduct e-commerce if appropriate. Although building a Web site takes money and effort, it's a business necessity. A recent study of small businesses that have a Web site found that 78 percent feel their business benefits by being online.[1]

Although building a Web site takes time, money, and effort, it's a business necessity.

Creating a Web site involves three key steps: determining the objectives of the site, building the site, and monitoring the site to assess and improve its effectiveness.

Determining the objectives of your Web site

There are many options regarding the look and functionality of a Web site, so it's important to determine what you want your Web site to accomplish before you start building it. There are basically three levels of Web sites to choose from[2]:

- Basic Web site—A basic Web site introduces your business and consists of a few pages that highlight your product or service, archive news releases and press about your business, and provide contact information. These sites are usually created from a template and cost as little as $200 if you build it yourself or between $1,000 and $3,000 if you hire someone else to do it.

■ Intermediate Web site—An intermediate site allows you to receive online requests, sell products via a shopping cart, process credit cards, and display more information than a basic site. These sites are customized by a Web site designer and cost between $1,500 and $6,000.

■ Advanced Web site—An advanced site does everything an intermediate site does along with complex tasks like tracking inventory and maintaining customer databases. These sites involved specialized programming and run $5,000 and up.

Building Your Web Site

If you're content with a basic Web site and have a limited budget, there are do-it-yourself Web site packages available through vendors such as Homestead (www.homestead.com) and Register.com (www.register.com). These companies sell packages that include instructions and tools for building a Web site, along with the services necessary to launch and maintain the site. If you don't want to do the work yourself, or you want an intermediate or advanced site, you'll have to hire a Web design firm.[3] One thing to be careful of is not to totally turn over the design and maintenance of your Web site to someone else. Although you may need a Web design firm to build and host your site, you should learn how to add content to your site and make changes on your own.

Many excellent books and periodicals talk about Web site design. You should consider several questions when building your site and on a periodic basis after it's up and running.

■ Is it visually appealing?

■ Do the pages load quickly?

■ Is the layout well organized?

■ Is it easy to navigate?

■ Does it answer the most obvious questions that someone coming to the site might have?

■ Is the site easy to find?

■ Does the site emphasize the points that differentiate my company from my competitors?

Monitoring your Web site to assess and improve its effectiveness

The third step in launching and maintaining a Web site is to monitor its effectiveness and make changes when necessary. This is an activity (called Web analytics) that many small businesses don't engage in. When you launch your site, you have to hire a company to host it. Make sure that your host is set up to give you statistics on the usage of your site, or hire a separate company to give you the information. A sample of the information you can obtain is as follows:

- The number of visitors you have each hour, day, and week of the month

- The number of unique visitors that you receive (on a daily or weekly basis)

- A report on where your visitors come from

- A report on what pages on your Web site are viewed the most frequently

- Statistics that track a sales campaign's effectiveness

By analyzing this type of information, you can see the pages and products that people are most interested in, whether there are a high number of people visiting a particular product page but not buying (indicating that the page needs to be reworked), and how well offline promotional campaigns are working. For example, if Helen's Grill ran a series of ads in a local newspaper, and it prominently displayed its Web site address in the ads, one way it could measure the success of the newspaper campaign is by monitoring the degree to which the ads increased traffic to its Web site.

TRUTH

21

How to think about money as it relates to starting a business

A concern that most prospective business owners have is whether they'll be able to raise sufficient funds to start a business. It's a legitimate concern. It does take money to start and grow a business. But the amount of money needed to start a specific business is not a set amount. The same business might cost one person $10,000 to start and another person $25,000—trust me, this isn't an exaggeration. The amount needed depends on how a person thinks about money as it relates to the start-up process, how frugal a person is, and how resourceful a person is in gaining access to money and other resources.

One of the reasons that many businesses are started for as little as they are is that people adjust their attitudes about money as they get acquainted with the start-up process.

The following are two categories of insights regarding the role of money in starting a business. As you read through these insights, think about your own attitudes about money. One of the reasons that many businesses are started for as little as they are is that people adjust their attitudes about money as they get acquainted with the start-up process.

Skimpy finances can be a blessing rather than a curse

The first category of insights regarding money and the start-up process is that there is a silver lining to having limited start-up funds. While Truths 23 through 27 focus on how to raise start-up funds, more people finance their start-ups with their own money than from bank loans, money from investors, or some other means.[1] Although this reality leaves many business owners with skimpy start-up funds, there is an upside. Many successful business owners, looking back, feel that having limited funds forced them to focus, become self-reliant, and develop a mindset of frugality—qualities that have served them well as they've grown their firms. This sentiment is affirmed by Caterina Fake, cofounder of Flickr, the popular photo-sharing Web site, which was started in 2002. In reflecting back on the role of money in the early days of her firm, Fake said:

> *"The money was scarce, but I'm a big believer that constraints inspire creativity. The less money you have, the fewer people and resources you have, the more creative you have to become. I think that had a lot to do with why we were able to iterate and innovate so fast."*[2]

There is another silver lining to launching a firm with limited funds. Although in some cases it is necessary to go to a bank or an investor to obtain financing, the problem with obtaining money from these sources is that there are consequences that business owners often don't fully anticipate. While most bankers and investors have good intentions, they assert considerable control over the businesses they provide money to as a means of protecting their investments. So for people leaving traditional jobs to start their own businesses, obtaining money from a banker or investor is often like trading one boss for another. You might free yourself from working for a boss in a traditional sense but could have an equally influential boss in the form of a banker or investor.

Techniques that enable business owners to minimize start-up costs

The second category of insights regarding money and the start-up process is that there are techniques that enable business owners to minimize the costs associated with starting a business. There are three predominant techniques.

The first technique is to select an appropriate business to start. If you have limited start-up funds, you should start a business that requires a small up-front investment. Fortunately, many businesses meet this criterion. Home-based businesses, which now represent more than half of the 26.8 million U.S. small businesses, are popular largely because they take very little capital to start. The second technique is to seek out help. For small business owners, there are many sources of assistance that provide counsel and advice on how to minimize start-up expenses. An example is the Service Corps of

Retired Executives (SCORE), which is a nonprofit organization that provides free consulting services to small business. There are also organizations that provide coaching and support to specific groups of business owners and tailor their offerings to fit the groups. An example is Ladies Who Launch, an organization that sponsors workshops and provides materials that encourage and inform female business owners.[3]

The third technique is to cut costs and save money at every opportunity. The most effective way to do this is to develop a mindset of frugality and resourcefulness. While many people aren't naturally frugal, they foster these qualities to get their businesses off the ground and to minimize the costs of their ongoing operations. Common money-saving techniques include buying used equipment instead of new, obtaining payments in advance from customers, and buying items cheaply but prudently through discount outlets or online auctions such as eBay, rather than at full-price stores.

22

Calculating your initial start-up costs

The first step in determining how much money it will take to start a specific business and whether you'll need to pursue outside financing is to determine your start-up costs. A business's start-up costs refer to the total cash needed to get the business up and running. All businesses incur expenses before they make their first sale. A common mistake that business owners make is to underestimate their start-up costs and get caught short on cash before their business even opens.

A common mistake that business owners make is to underestimate their start-up costs and get caught short on cash before their business even opens.

How to calculate your start-up costs

Prepare a budget that lists all the costs that you'll incur to launch your business. You need to consider four categories of costs.

- **Capital costs**—This category includes real estate, buildings, equipment, vehicles, furniture, fixtures (shelves, wall brackets, cabinets), and similar capital purchases. These costs vary considerably depending on the business. A restaurant or retail store may have substantial initial capital costs, while a home-business may have little to no capital expenses.

- **"One-time" expenses**—This category includes legal expenses, fees for businesses licenses and permits, deposits for utilities, Web site design, business logo design, and similar one-time expenses and fees. All businesses incur at least some of these expenses.

- **Provisions for initial operating losses**—Many businesses require a ramp-up period in which they lose money until they are fully up to steam and reach profitability. For example, it usually takes a new fitness center several months to reach its membership goals. It's important to have cash set aside to make it through this period. If you have a business plan, and the plan includes pro forma (or projected) financial statements, you should have an accurate estimate of your initial losses. If you don't have a business plan, experts recommend that you set aside six months of your business's estimated monthly operating expenses to see you through the ramp-up period. You'll need to estimate your monthly operating expenses to arrive at this figure.

- **Provisions for living expenses**—Experts also recommend that you set aside six months of living expenses for you and your family to see you through the ramp-up period. The need to do this depends on your individual situation. Some business owners have spouses who are working that can cover their living expenses. Other businesses start part-time, and the business owner keeps his or her full-time job until the business is cash-flow positive.

Don't get caught unaware regarding start-up expenses. It is better to overestimate rather than underestimate the amount it will cost to launch your business, and adding a cushion is a good idea. Murphy's Law is prevalent in the start-up world—things will go wrong. It is a rare start-up that doesn't experience some unexpected expenses during the start-up phase.

Finding information on start-up costs

You need to estimate start-up costs as accurately as possible. There are several ways of finding the information you need, all of which involve a little legwork. You can estimate your expenses item by item by contacting the appropriate vendors, government agencies, and people who can provide informed estimates. For example, if you're thinking about leasing space in a strip mall, you can usually obtain data on what strip mall space goes for from a local realtor or property manager. Another way to identify start-up costs is to talk to the owners of businesses that are similar to the one that you're planning to start. You should try to find businesses that are outside your trade area so the owners don't see you as a potential competitor. Many first-time business owners are surprised by how cooperative and helpful other business owners are. Another approach is to contact a trade association that represents businesses in the industry you'll be entering. Many trade associations compile statistics on start-up costs. There are also online resources that help business owners connect with people who are eager to help. For example, Startup Nation (www.startupnation.com) is an online community that allows business owners to connect with one another and chat about start-up costs and other business-related topics.

Determining the financing that you'll need

Once you know what your start-up costs will be, you'll be in a position to determine the most appropriate way to finance or fund your business.

Once you know what your start-up costs will be, you'll be in a position to determine the most appropriate way to finance your business. The five ways to finance a new business include (1) personal funds (including loans from friends and family and bootstrapping), (2) debt financing, (3) equity funding, (4) grants, and (5) other potential sources of financing. These sources are discussed in Truths 23 to 27.

23

Personal funds, loans from friends and family, and bootstrapping

The most common source of start-up funds is the founder's personal savings.[1] This source is closely followed by loans from friends and family and personal sources of debt, such as credit cards and home equity loans. If you're surprised by these statements, you're not alone. There is a prevailing belief that most business owners must appeal to bankers or investors to get their businesses off the ground. Some businesses do require bank loans or money from investors to get started, but the majority of business owners rely on personal funds, loans from friends and family, personal sources of debt, and bootstrapping to get started.

This Truth focuses on loans from friends and family and boostrapping as two common ways of raising start-up funds. Both of these choices can be great sources of start-up funds, but you need to utilize them in ways that maintain positive family relationships and allow a business to reach its full potential. Personal sources of debt, such as credit cards and home equity loans, are discussed in Truth 24, "Debt financing."

> The most common source of start-up funds is the founder's personal savings. This source is closely followed by loans from friends and family.

Loans from friends and family

According to the Global Entrepreneurship Monitor, which is a joint research effort by Babson College and the London Business School, millions of businesses are financed each year with money from friends and family, while only a few thousand obtain funds from professional investors. In fact, in the United States, from 2000 to 2003, 5 percent of the adult population invested privately in some else's business. The investment went to close family members (41.8 percent), friends and neighbors (28.5 percent), other relatives (10.5 percent), strangers (9.4 percent), work colleagues (6.1 percent), and other (3.6 percent).[2] Besides offering loans, friends and family often help out new business owners with gifts, forgone or delayed compensation (if a friend or family member works for the new business), or reduced or free rent. For example, Cisco Systems, the giant producer of Internet-related gear, started out in the house of one of its cofounder's parents.

There are three rules of thumb that you should follow when asking friends and family members for start-up funds. First, you should present your request in a businesslike manner, just like you would to a banker or investor. Describe the potential of the business along with the risks involved. Second, if the help you receive is in the form of a loan, a promissory note should be prepared, with a repayment schedule, and the note should be signed by both parties. Stipulating the terms of the loan in writing reduces the potential of a misunderstanding and protects both you and the friend or family member providing the funding. Third, you should be careful to ask only people for help who are in a legitimate position to offer assistance. It's not a good idea to ask certain friends or family members, regardless of how much they may have expressed a willingness to help, for assistance if losing the money would cripple them financially. Remember, there are risks involved with any new business. If you're unable to repay a loan to a friend or family member, you risk not only damaging your business relationship with them but your personal relationship as well.

> You should be careful to ask only people for help who are in a legitimate position to offer assistance.

Bootstrapping

Bootstrapping is finding ways to raise start-up funds without the need for external funds through creativity, ingenuity, thriftiness, or any means necessary.[3] (The term comes from the adage "pull yourself up by the bootstraps.") It is the term attached to the general philosophy of minimizing start-up expenses by aggressively pursuing costs-cutting techniques and money-saving tactics, as discussed in Truth 21, "How to think about money as it relates to business." There are many well-known examples of business owners who bootstrapped to get their companies started. Legend has it that Steve Jobs and partner Steve Wozniak sold a Volkswagen van and a

Hewlett-Packard programmable calculator to raise $1,350, which was the initial seed capital for Apple, Inc.

While bootstrapping is highly recommended in almost all start-up situations, there are subtle downsides. Cost-cutting and saving money are admirable practices, but if you push these practices too far, you can hold a business back from reaching its full potential. In addition, business owners who bootstrap by working out of their homes rather than renting office space are often lonely. The price of renting space in an office building or strip mall where there are other businesses present may be worth it if it provides a business owner access to a network of people who can be relied on to provide social support and business advice.

TRUTH

24

Debt financing

About 48 percent of businesses use some form of debt financing during their initial year of operation. The sources most frequently used are personal credit card debt (30.2 percent), personal bank loans (18 percent), business credit card debt (14.6 percent), and loans from friends and family (10.1 percent).[1] Note that the majority of debt financing is not in the form of a bank loan. Instead, business owners rely on more personal sources of debt financing to supplement their start-up needs.

The majority of debt financing is not in the form of a bank loan. Instead, business owners must rely on more personal sources of debt financing to supplement their start-up needs.

There are two major advantages to debt financing opposed to equity funding, which will be discussed in Truth 25, "Equity funding." The first is that none of the ownership of the business is surrendered—a major advantage for most business owners. The second is that interest payments on a loan (in most cases) are tax deductible, in contrast to dividend payments made to investors, which aren't. There are two major disadvantages to debt financing. The first is that debt must be repaid. Cash is typically tight during a start-up's first few months and sometimes for a year or more. The second is that lenders often impose strict conditions on loans and insist on ample collateral to fully protect their investment. This often requires that a business owner's personal assets be collateralized as a condition of the loan.

Commercial banks are not a practical source of financing for most new businesses.[2] This sentiment isn't a knock against banks; it's just that banks are risk adverse, and financing start-ups is a risky business. That's not to say that you can't get a home equity loan to fund part or all of your start-up needs. It's just that most banks won't normally assume the risk of loaning money directly to a business with an unproven track record. They would rather loan money to an individual who has equity in a home to pledge as collateral.

When banks do loan money to start-ups, the money is often loaned through the Small Business Administration (SBA) Guaranteed Loan Program. This program is a realistic alternative for many start-ups and offers reduced interest rates and longer repayment terms than conventional loans. The SBA does not have money to lend but makes it easier for business owners to obtain loans from banks by guaranteeing the loans. The most notable SBA program available to small businesses is the 7(A) Loan Guaranty Program. The loans are for small businesses that are not able to obtain loans on reasonable terms through normal lending channels. Almost all small businesses are eligible to apply for an SBA guaranteed loan. The SBA can guarantee as much as 85 percent on loans up to $150,000 and 75 percent on loans over $150,000. In most cases, the maximum guarantee is $1.5 million. A guaranteed loan can be used for working capital to start a new business or expand an existing one. It can also be used for real estate purchases, renovation, construction, or equipment purchases. The best way to learn more about the SBA Guaranteed Loan Program and determine if you are eligible is to meet with a participating lender.

There are a variety of other avenues that business owners can pursue to borrow money. Getting loans from friends and family, as discussed in Truth 23, "Personal loans, loans from friends and family, and bootstrapping," is a popular choice. Credit card debt, although easy to obtain, should be used sparingly. One channel for borrowing funds that is getting quite a bit of attention is Prosper.com, a peer-to-peer lending network. Prosper is an online auction Web site that matches people who want to borrow money with people who are willing to make loans. Most of the loans made via Prosper are fairly small ($25,000) but might be sufficient to meet a new business's needs.[3] There are also organizations that lend money to specific demographic groups. For example, Count Me In, an advocacy group for female business owners, provides loans of $500 to $10,000 to women starting or growing

> One channel for borrowing funds that is getting quite a bit of attention is Prosper.com, a peer-to-peer lending network.

a business.[4] An organization that is aligned with Count Me In and American Express, named Make Mine a Million $ Business, lends up to $50,000 to female-owned start-ups that have been in business for at least two years and have $250,000 or more in annual revenue.[5]

Some lenders specialize in *microfinancing*, which are very small loans. For example, Accion USA gives $500 credit-builder loans to people with no credit history.[6] While $500 might not sound like much, it could be enough to open a home-based business such as an eBay Store or to get started in a direct sales organization.

TRUTH

25

Equity funding

Equity funding is obtaining money from an investor. Investors are typically interested in businesses that plan to grow and can capture fairly large markets. These businesses normally have a unique business idea and a proven management team and are shooting to capture large markets. If your business fits this profile, and you're willing to accept the hectic pace of activity that running a rapid growth business entails, seeking equity funding may be a good option for your business.

The primary advantage of equity funding is access to capital, which is the reason it's often pursued by businesses that have high start-up costs. In addition, because investors become partial owners of the firms they invest in, they often try to help those firms by offering their expertise and assistance. The money received from investors also doesn't have to be paid back. The investor receives a return on the investment through dividend payments and by selling the stock. The primary disadvantage of equity funding is that the firm's owners relinquish part of their ownership interest and may lose some control.

There are two sources of equity funding: business angels and venture capitalists.

> The primary advantage of equity funding is access to capital, which is the reason it's often pursued by businesses that have high start-up costs.

Business angels

Business angels are individuals who directly invest their personal funds into start-ups. They generally invest between $10,000 and $500,000 in a single company and are looking for companies that have the potential to grow 30 to 40 percent per year (which is very aggressive) before they are acquired or go public.[1] Jeffrey Sohl, the director of the University of New Hampshire's Center for Venture Research, estimates that only 10 percent to 15 percent of private companies meet that criterion.[2] The one exception that might help you get your foot in the door with an angel investor, if your business doesn't meet the traditional criteria, is if the purpose of your business is aligned with a personal interest or passion of the investor. For instance, if you're starting a company to make a safer car seat for infant children and meet an angel investor who has an intense interest in child safety products, you could capture the investor's attention even if your firm isn't capable of a 30 to 40 percent per year growth rate.

Most business angels remain fairly anonymous and are matched up with business owners through referrals. If you're interested in pursuing angel funding, you should discretely work your network of acquaintances (bankers, lawyers, accountants, successful entrepreneurs) to see if anyone can make an appropriate introduction.

Venture capitalists

The second type of equity investor is venture capitalists. Venture capital firms are limited partnerships of money managers who raise money in "funds" to invest in start-ups and growing firms. Some of the better-known venture capital firms are Kleiner Perkins, Sequoia Capital, and Redpoint Ventures. Similar to business angels, venture capital firms look for a 30 to 40 percent annual return on their investments and a total return over the life of investments of 5 to 20 times the initial investments. The major difference between venture capital firms and business angels is that venture capital firms lend little money to start-ups (preferring to wait until a firm proves its product and market) and normally don't

> The major difference between venture capital firms and business angels is that venture capital firms lend little money to start-ups and normally don't invest less than $1 million in a single firm.

invest less than $1 million in a single firm. As a result, venture capital funding is only practical for a small number of business start-ups.

TRUTH

26

Grants: It takes the right fit

A potential source of small business funding is grants. A grant is a gift of money that does not have to be repaid. While there is no nationwide network for awarding grants to start-up firms, almost every state, city, and local community is trying to find ways to encourage people to start businesses as a way of growing their economies. As a result, there are a growing number of programs available through both the public and the private sectors to provide grant money to promising business start-ups.

Obtaining a grant takes a little detective work. Granting agencies are by nature low-key, so they normally need to be sought out. The best place to inquire about the availability of grants for a particular business is via your local Small Business Development Center, SCORE chapter, and similar organizations. Although these groups rarely have grant money available, they'll be able to direct you to organizations that are awarding grants to small businesses in your area. Most grant programs are competitive, meaning that you have to apply for the grant and compete against other start-ups to receive the funds. One of the keys to obtaining grants is to learn to write effective grant proposals. Many Small Business Development Centers sponsor seminars on how to write successful proposals.

> Obtaining a grant takes a little detective work. Granting agencies are by nature low-key, so they normally need to be sought out.

A typical scenario of a small business that received a grant is provided by Rozalia Williams, the founder of Hidden Curriculum Education, a for-profit company that offers college life skills courses. To kick-start her business, Williams received a $72,500 grant from Miami Dade Empowerment Trust, a granting agency in Dade County, Florida. The purpose of the Miami Dade Empowerment Trust is to encourage the creation of businesses in disadvantaged neighborhoods of Dade County. The key to William's success, which is true in most grant-awarding situations, is that her business fit nicely with the mission of the granting organization, and she was willing to take her business into the areas the granting agency was committed to improving. After being awarded the grant and conducting her college prep courses in four Dade County neighborhoods over a three-year period, Williams received an additional $100,000 loan from the Miami Dade Empowerment Trust to expand her business.[1] There are also private foundations that grant money to both existing and start-up firms. These grants are generally tied to specific objectives or a specific project, such as research and development in a specific industry.

The federal government has a pair of grant programs for technology firms. The Small Business Innovation Research (SBIR) program is an established program that provides over $1 billion in cash grants per year to small businesses that are working on projects in specific areas. Each year, ten federal departments and agencies are required by SBIR to reserve a portion of their research and development funds for awards to small businesses. The second program, Small Business Technology Transfer (STTR), is similar to the SBIR program except it requires the participation of researchers working at universities or other research institutions. A list of the agencies that participate in both programs, along with an explanation of the application processes, is available at www.sba.gov/SBIR.

The full spectrum of grants available through the federal government is listed at www.grants.gov. State and local governments, private foundations, and philanthropic organizations also post grants announcements on their Web sites. Finding a grant that fits your business is the key. This is no small task. It is worth the effort, however, if you can obtain some or all of your start-up costs through a granting agency.

Finding a grant that fits your business is the key. This is no small task.

One thing to be careful of is grant-related scams. As a business owner, you may receive unsolicited e-mail messages from individuals or organizations that assure you that for a fee they can help you gain access to hundreds of business-related grants. The reality is that there aren't hundreds of grants that fit any one business—so the offer is likely a scam.

TRUTH

27

Persistence pays off: Finding alternative sources of start-up funds

There are sources of funds for new businesses that aren't as obvious as traditional sources of debt financing, equity funding, and grants. A mistake that people make when looking for start-up funds is not casting their net wide enough. It's also a mistake to place too much reliance on a single source of financing without considering alternatives.

Similar to finding grants, finding obscure sources of financing takes legwork and persistence. In most cases, you must also match your start-up with a program or source of funding that fits the nature of your business. The following is a partial list of sources to consider. The best way to become aware of these and similar sources is to work your network of business acquaintances. Many sources of start-up funds fly just under the radar. The most common way to learn about them is through a tip or a referral from a business associate.

> Many sources of start-up funds fly just under the radar. The most common way to learn about them is through a tip or a referral from a business associate.

Business plan competitions and other contests

An increasing number of business plan competitions are held across the United States. Many of these competitions offer cash prizes. The number of small business contests sponsored by companies that sell products to small businesses is also increasing. An example is the VISA Business Breakthrough Contest, a joint venture between VISA and MSN, which in 2007 offered five $10,000 awards to businesses that submitted essays explaining how they became more efficient in one of five categories (finance, marketing, organization, team building, and technology).[1] A simple Google search using the keywords "small business contests" will produce similar examples.

State and community small business loan and assistance programs

Many state and community not-for-profit organizations and governmental agencies sponsor loan programs designed to encourage and support business ownership. An example is the Vermont Community Loan Fund, which is a fund that provides loans to businesses that help revitalize struggling communities in Vermont and provide jobs to low-to-moderate-income Vermonters.[2] A similar example is the First Community Loan Fund in Delaware. The fund is a not-for-profit Community Development Financial Institution (CDFI) that specializes in supporting small businesses, micro-enterprises, and affordable housing in the State of Delaware.[3] The best way to find if there are equivalent programs in your state is to check with your local Small Business Development Center or your state Department of Commerce.

Patriot Express Pilot Loan Initiative

The Patriot Express Pilot Loan Initiative is a program sponsored by the Small Business Administration (SBA) to help veterans and members of the military community gain access to the resources needed to start a business. It's the only program sponsored by the SBA that targets a specific group of people. Similar to the SBA Guaranteed Loan Program discussed in Truth 24, "Debt financing," the initiative does not lend money directly to veterans but makes it easier for veterans to obtain financing by guaranteeing loans offered by the SBA's network of participating lenders. It features the SBA's lowest interest rates for guaranteed business loans. The program extends to spouses of active duty military personnel and the widowed spouses of service members who died during service or of a service-connected disability.[4]

Loan and grant programs for women and minority business owners

There are a growing number of business assistance programs that target women and minority business owners. For example, the Minority Business Development Agency (MBDA) is a federal agency created specifically to foster the establishment and growth of minority-owned businesses. MBDA provides funding for Minority Business Development Centers, Native American Business Development Centers, and Business Resource Centers located throughout the United States. While these centers are not a direct source of start-up funds, they provide assistance in many areas and help minority-owned businesses seek financing through a variety of channels.[5] An example of an organization set up to invest money in minority businesses is the Minority Angel Investor Network (MAIN). It is a network of accredited investors with an interest and commitment to invest in high-growth, minority-owned, or minority-led companies. The organization's focus is on businesses in the greater Philadelphia, Pennsylvania area.[6]

Customer and supplier financing

Customers and suppliers are an often-overlooked source of start-up financing. Sometimes suppliers, if they recognize that your business has the potential to become a regular customer, will provide your business financing or funding to help it get off the ground. Similarly, if you feel that your product or service will add considerable value for a particular customer and save the customer money, the customer might be willing to prepurchase a certain amount of the product, which is a way for you to generate start-up funds. If you're buying a franchise, you can typically obtain financing through your franchisor.

Tapping into personal funds

There are also ways that business owners tap into personal funds to raise start-up capital, beyond using savings and cash on hand. Examples include borrowing against the cash value of a life insurance policy and tapping into an IRA, 401K, or similar retirement account. You'll normally need guidance and advice from a tax accountant to draw funds from a tax-deferred retirement account to finance a business venture.

TRUTH

28

How to approach the task of building a "new business" team

One facet of starting a business that all experts agree on is that the quality of the people who start and build a business is instrumental to its success. As one expert put it, "People are the one factor in production...that animates all the others.[1] Often, several businesses are started at the same time that sell essentially the same product or service. When this happens, the key to success is not the product or service but rather the ability of the initial founder or founders to assemble a team that can execute the idea better than anyone else.

A new business's "team" is the group of founders, key employees, and advisers that move a new business from an idea to a fully functioning firm. Usually, the team doesn't come together all at once. Instead, it is built as the new business grows and can afford to hire additional personnel. The team also involves more than paid employees. Many new businesses have a board of directors, a board of advisors, and other professionals they rely on for direction and advice.

There are two issues that you should be particularly sensitive to as you build your team. Your sensitivity to these issues and the way you handle them will send important signals to the people who you'll approach for access to resources (such as bankers and investors) and will be instrumental to the way in which your new business team takes shape.

A new business's "team" is the group of founders, key employees, and advisers that move a new business from an idea to a fully functioning firm.

Being open to advice

First, the way your new business team is put together indicates the extent to which you're open to advice and are able to generate enthusiasm for your business. If you start a business and are relying strictly on yourself, you run the risk of conveying to others that you are a "one-man show" and have no intentions of building a team or taking advice from others. In contrast, if you start a business and report that you've attended a number of small business seminars, have met with counselors from your local Small Business Develop

Center and SCORE chapter, and have a five-member advisory board already in place, you're conveying a very different impression. These efforts show that you're open to advice, are willing to share power, and are able to garner support for your business idea. These initiatives may also cause a banker or investor to think, "Wow, if this person ever gets in a bind, he or she'll have a nice network to lean on for counsel and advice," or "If this person is able to fill a five-member advisory board before his or her business even starts, I bet he or she will have no trouble selling the business concept to paying customers."

> The way your new business team is assembled indicates the extent to which you're open to advice and able to generate enthusiasm for your business.

Having a clear sense of how the business will evolve

The second thing to be sensitive to as you start building your new business team is to have a clear sense of how the team will evolve. Almost all new businesses have gaps in the personnel they need. That's normal. Just make sure you have a plausible explanation for how you're dealing with the gaps until you can permanently fill them. In addition, avoid the impression that you're naïve or unsure about the order in which to fill the gaps. For example, if you're developing a new product, such as an accessory for the Apple iPhone, you'll need access to expertise on marketing and sales during the time the product is being developed, to make sure it's saleable after it's produced. For you to say that a marketing and salesperson will be hired after the product is developed shows a lack of understanding of the proper upfront role of marketing input. If you can't afford to hire a marketing person during your product development stage, that's understandable, but evidence should be provided that shows where you'll get access to marketing expertise. This is where aligning yourself with a competent SCORE advisor, establishing a relationship with your local Small Business Development Center, or putting together a board of directors or a board of advisors plays a vital role.

You can often mine one or more of these groups, usually for free, to find people with specific expertise who are willing to provide counsel and advice until you can afford to hire full-time expertise.

TRUTH

29

Starting a business as a team rather than an individual

One of the most significant decisions a prospective business owner makes is whether to launch a business as a sole proprietor or whether to take on one or more partners. There is no best choice that works in all situations. The choice normally boils down to whether the idea for the business was conceived with others and whether the people involved are equally committed to starting a business.

While most businesses are started as sole proprietorships, a growing number of businesses are started by a team of two or more people.[1] Businesses that fit this criterion must organize as a partnership, corporation, or limited liability company. It's normally not a good idea to organize as a general partnership, because the individual partners are liable for all the partnership's obligations. This complication can be overcome by organizing as a corporation or a limited liability company, as described in Truth 19, "Choosing a form of business ownership." It's best to have an attorney involved to help you navigate the legalese of starting a business with two or more people, to make sure you select a form of business ownership that meets your collective goals.

Most founding teams consist of two to four people. A team larger than four people is typically too big to be practical.[2]

Advantages to starting as a team rather than an individual

It's generally believed that new businesses started by a team have an advantage over those started by an individual. A team brings more talent, resources, ideas, and professional contacts to a new business than does a sole proprietor.[3] In addition, the psychological support that cofounders of a new business can offer one another may be an important element in a firm's success.

It's generally believed that new businesses started by a team have an advantage over those started by an individual.

Several factors affect the value of a team that is starting a new business. First, teams that have worked together before have an advantage. If people have worked together before and have decided to partner to start a business together, it usually means that they get along personally and trust one another.[4] They also tend to communicate with one another more effectively than people who are new to one another.[5] Second, if the members of the team are diverse in terms of their abilities and experiences, they are likely to have different points of view about technology, hiring decisions, and other issues. Typically, these different points of view generate debate among the founders, reducing the likelihood that decisions will be made in haste or without the airing of alternative points of view.

Disadvantages to starting as a team rather than an individual

There are two potential disadvantages associated with starting a business as a team rather than as a sole business owner. First, the team members may not get along. This is why investors and others favor teams consisting of people who have worked together before. Second, if two or more people start a business as "equals," conflicts can arise when the business needs to establish a formal structure and designate one person as the chief executive officer (CEO). If the business has investors, the investors will usually weigh in on who should be appointed CEO. In these instances, it's easy for the founder who wasn't chosen as the CEO to feel slighted. This problem is exacerbated if multiple founders are involved. At some point, a hierarchy will have to be developed, and the founders will have to decide who reports to whom.

Founders' agreement

One of the smartest things a team of founders can do to avoid the pitfalls identified in the previous section is to draft a founders' agreement before the business is started. A founders' agreement is a document that deals with issues such as the relative split of the equity among the founders of the firm and how individual founders will be compensated for the cash or the "sweat equity" they put into the firm.[6] The items typically included in a well-developed founders' agreement are as follows:

115

- Nature of the prospective business
- A brief business plan
- Proposed titles of the individual founders
- Apportionment of stock (or division of ownership)
- Identification of any intellectual property signed over to the business by any of the founders
- Buyback clause, which explains how a founder's shares will be disposed of if he or she dies, wants to sell, or is forced to sell by court order

Having a founders' agreement ensures that the founders have addressed and hashed out critical issues regarding their respective roles in the business before the business is started.

TRUTH

30

Recruiting and hiring employees

New businesses vary in terms of how quickly they need to recruit and hire employees. In some instances, the founder or founders work alone until the business generates enough sales to justify hiring the first hourly or salaried employees. In other instances, employees are hired immediately.

Founders differ in their approach to the task of recruiting and selecting employees. Some founders draw on their network of contacts to identify candidates. Others advertise their openings through traditional media such as classified ads and employment Web sites like Monster.com. One thing that surprises many first-

One thing that surprises many first-time business owners is that finding good employees is not an easy task.

time business owners is that finding good employees is not an easy task. In fact, several studies have shown that a difficulty in finding qualified employees is a barrier to growth for many new businesses.[1] As a result, you need to develop a deliberate and determined approach to recruiting and hiring and realize that finding good people takes time and effort.

Hiring your first employee

For many business owners, hiring the first employee is a milestone event. If the decision is prudent, it generally indicates that the business is gaining momentum. There are three rules of thumb for hiring your first employee that you should observe in most instances.

- Formalize the process by preparing a job description and conducting formal interviews for the position that is open. Give the position a title, and make sure you have a clear notion of the employee's authority and scope of responsibility.

- Comply with all the legal ramifications of becoming an employer by following IRS regulations regarding income tax withholdings from employee paychecks and similar matters. Also check with your state government to determine the documents you must file and whether you are required to pay worker's compensation insurance.

■ Pay a fair wage. Many small business owners are successful because they are willing to work extremely long hours for relatively low pay. The payoff comes through the increased valuation of the business.

For many business owners, hiring the first employee is a milestone event.

Unless you're willing to give your first employee an ownership stake in the business, you must pay a fair wage and set a reasonable work schedule to keep the employee.

Fortunately, there are many sources of assistance to help small business owners' work through the process of hiring their first employee. Small Business Development Centers sponsor workshops to teach strategies for recruiting and hiring employees. In most areas, they also make available "document packets" for employers who are hiring employees. The packets contain everything from tax forms to instructions on how to conduct background checks to drug testing forms. The IRS maintains a Web site to help small businesses understand the regulations they are required to comply with. It even offers online classes to explain the rules.[2] Many state governments maintain Web sites and distribute printed publications to help employers comply with state regulations.

Hiring tips and techniques

One hiring technique that many small businesses find useful is to try people out on a part-time basis or as a freelance employee (or intern) to determine if they are a good fit before offering them a full-time job. Individuals who are willing to work on a freelance basis, some of whom are looking for full-time jobs, can normally be identified through your personal network of acquaintances or through a freelance job-search Web site such as Guru.com or Elance.com.

An important tip for hiring employees is to be cautious about offering employees ownership interest in your business. The rationale for offering employees a piece of the company is to incent them to work hard and act like an owner. It's often not necessary to do this. If you can offer your early employees many of the same benefits you obtain from self-employment—a flexible schedule, the chance to work in an area they are passionate about, and freedom from the pressures associated with "climbing the corporate ladder"—you are in most instances already offering them a better experience than they would find through working for a midsized or large firm. If you do offer your employees an ownership interest in your business, make sure to vest theirs interests gradually. It's fully appropriate to require your employees to "earn" their ownership interest in your business through their performance and their longevity with the company.

TRUTH

31

Board of directors

The need for a board of directors depends on the type of business you start. If your business starts as a corporation, it is legally required to have a board of directors. A board of directors is a panel of individuals elected by a corporation's shareholders to oversee the management of the firm. In an early-stage firm or a small firm, the board may be restricted to the principles running the firm. In these instances, the board serves little more than a legal function. In other instances, however, the board plays an active role in the management and oversight of the business.

Technically, a board of directors has three responsibilities: (1) appoint the firm's officers, (2) declare dividends, and (3) oversee the affairs of the corporation. The optimal size of a board of directors for a start-up is three to five people.[1] A board is typically made up of both inside directors and outside directors. An inside director is also an officer of the firm. An outside director is someone who is not employed by the firm. A five-member board of directors usually consists of two inside directors and three outside directors. Most boards meet formally three or four times a year. Large firms pay their directors for their service. New businesses are more likely to pay their directors in company stock or ask them to serve without direct compensation—at least until the company is profitable.

If handled properly, a business's board of directors can be a central part of its new business team.

If handled properly, a business's board of directors can be a central part of its new business team. An active board provides guidance and lends legitimacy to a firm.

Provide guidance

Although a board of directors has formal oversight responsibility, its most useful role is to provide guidance and support to the managers of the firm. Many well-intended business founders and managers simply "don't know what they don't know," which often results in missteps early in the life of a start-up. Experienced board members often see these potential missteps before they occur and help new business teams avoid them. Many business owners interact with their board members frequently and obtain vital input. The key to making this happen is to select board members with needed skills and useful experience who are willing to give advice and ask insightful and probing questions.

Individual members of a board of directors can also help fill competency gaps when a company is started, as mentioned in Truth 28, "How to approach the task of building a 'new business' team." If a firm gets investment capital, the investor normally occupies a seat on its board of directors. Investors do this not only to protect their investment but also to assume a formal role in lending advice and assistance to the business.

Although a board of directors has formal oversight responsibility, its most useful role is to provide guidance and support to the managers of the firm.

Lend legitimacy

Providing legitimacy for a firm is another main function of a board of directors. Well-known and respected board members bring instant credibility to the firm. For example, just imagine the positive buzz a firm could generate if it could say that a well-known entrepreneur, investor, or banker had agreed to serve on its board of directors. This phenomenon is referred to a signaling. Presumably, a high-quality individual would be reluctant to serve on the board of a low-quality start-up because that would put his or her reputation at risk. So when a high-quality individual does agree to serve on the board of a new firm, the individual is in essence "signaling" that the company has the potential to be successful.[2]

Achieving legitimacy through high-quality board members can result in other positive outcomes. Well-known board members can often help companies get their foot in the door with potential suppliers and customers. Board members are also often instrumental in helping young firms arrange financing or funding.

TRUTH

32

Board of advisors

A board of advisors is a panel of experts asked by a firm's managers to provide counsel and advice on an ongoing basis. Unlike a board of directors, a board of advisors possesses no legal responsibility for the firm and gives nonbinding advice.[1] A board of advisors can be established for general purposes or can be set up to address a specific issue or need. For example, some start-ups set up customer advisory boards shortly after they are founded to help them fine-tune their initial offerings.

Similar to a board of directors, the main purposes of a board of advisors is to provide guidance and lend legitimacy to a firm. Both of these attributes are seen in the advisory board set up by Laura Udall, the entrepreneur who started ZUCA, a company that makes backpacks on rollers for school age kids. When asked about the types of advice and support she gets from people outside her immediate management team, Udall said,

> A board of advisors can be established for general purposes or can be set up to address a specific issue or need.

"The company has a board of directors, but I also have created a wonderful board of volunteer advisors that has been very helpful with tactical and strategic decisions. The advisory board has evolved over the years as a result of my network. I asked each of the members to join as a result of their specific expertise. It now includes a CFO/COO of a prominent corporation, an executive in the luggage industry, a mom inventor who has founded several successful companies, a product designer, and a manufacturing expert."[2]

Imagine the type of advice and support Udall gleans from this group of advisors.

Most boards of advisors have between 5 and 15 members and interact with each other and with a firm's managers in several ways. Some advisory boards meet three or four times a year at the company's offices or in another location. Other advisory boards meet in an online environment. In some cases, a firm's board of advisors are scattered across the country, making it more cost-effective for a business's owners to interact with the members of the board on the telephone or via e-mail rather than bring them together physically. In these situations, board members don't interact with each other on a face-to-face basis, yet they still provide high levels of counsel and advice. The fact that a start-up has a board of directors does not preclude it from establishing one or more advisory boards. For example, Coolibar, a maker of sun protective clothing, has a board of directors and a medical advisory board. According to Coolibar, its medical advisory board "provides advice to the company regarding UV radiation, sunburn, and the science of detecting, preventing, and treating skin cancer and other UV-related medical disorders, such as lupus."[3] The board currently consists of six medical doctors, all with impressive credentials. Similarly, Intouch Technologies, a medical robotics companies, has a board of directors along with a business and strategy advisory board, an application and clinical advisory board, and a scientific and technical advisory board.[4]

The fact that a start-up has a board of directors does not preclude it from establishing one or more advisory boards.

   Although having a board of advisors is widely recommended in start-up circles, most start-ups do not have one. As a result, one way you can make your start-up stand out is to have one or more boards of advisors.

TRUTH

33

Intellectual property: What is it, and how is it protected?

Imagine that you have started a business to produce a new type of smoke alarm that is specifically designed for kitchens. It is similar to other smoke alarms but is more capable of detecting a kitchen fire than any alarm on the market. You've named it "Kitchen Sentry." Your tagline is "We Protect Cooks and Kitchens." You just acquired the Internet domain name www.kitchensentryfirmalarm.com.

Fortunately, during the time you were developing your product, you attended a seminar on intellectual property sponsored by your local Small Business Development Center (SBDC). You immediately went to an attorney who specializes in helping small businesses secure their intellectual property to talk about your device. Since that time, you have applied for a patent; trademarked the "Kitchen Sentry" name, your tagline, and your logo; and copyrighted key portions of your printed material. You have also designated certain portions of what you do as trade secrets. For example, the software code that helps the Kitchen Sentry detect a kitchen fire earlier than any other firm alarm is not protected by a patent. It's nearly impossible for a competitor to learn the code by reverse-engineering one of your devices. As a result, rather than disclosing this information, which would be necessary if you patented it, you have decided to keep it secret and protect it internally.

Like Kitchen Sentry, many new businesses have valuable intellectual property. *Intellectual property* is any product of human intellect that is intangible but has value in the marketplace. Traditionally, businesses have thought of their physical assets—such as land, buildings, and

Intellectual property is any product of human intellect that is intangible but has value in the marketplace.

equipment—as their most important assets. Increasingly, however, a business's intellectual assets are the most valuable. Think of the value of the Starbuck's trademark, the Nike "swoosh" logo, or the Microsoft Windows operating system. All of these are examples of intellectual property that provide their respective businesses with a competitive advantage in the marketplace. A business like Nike would be hurt much more by the loss of its "swoosh" logo than by the loss of a physical asset such as a building or piece of equipment.

The four forms of intellectual property protection are patents, trademarks, copyrights, and trade secrets. They are described in Truths 34 to 37. Intellectual property laws exist to encourage individuals and businesses to be innovative and to take risks by granting them exclusive rights to the fruits of their labors for a period of time. There would be no financial incentive for an individual to invent a device, like the Kitchen Sentry firm alarm, if it could be immediately copied by someone else. Intellectual property laws also help individuals make well-informed choices. For example, when consumers see a Panera Bread restaurant, they know exactly what to expect because only Panera Bread is permitted to use the Panera Bread trademark for soups, signature sandwiches, and bakery products.

A business like Nike would be hurt much more by the loss of its "swoosh" logo than by the loss of a physical asset such as a building or piece of equipment.

One special note about intellectual property laws is that it's up to business owners to take advantage of them and to safeguard their intellectual property once it is legally protected. Police forces and fire departments are available to quickly respond if a business owner's buildings or physical assets are threatened, but there are no intellectual property police forces or fire departments in existence. The courts prosecute individuals and companies that break intellectual property laws. However, it is up to the individual business owner to understand intellectual property laws, safeguard intellectual property assets, and initiate litigation if intellectual property rights are infringed upon or violated.

TRUTH

34

To patent or not to patent?

When it comes to inventing a product, like the new type of fire alarm described in Truth 33, "Intellectual property: What is it, and how is it protected?" the first thing you should do is get a patent, right? Well, maybe. Getting a patent is an expensive and time-consuming process. As a result, while there are many good reasons for getting a patent, there are several steps you should take before hiring a patent attorney and starting the process.

Steps to take before applying for a patent

First, as discussed in Truth 9, "Screening and testing business ideas," you should test and screen your business idea to make sure it has value in the marketplace. A common mistake that business owners make is to invent a product, spend a considerable amount and money to patent it, and find that the market for the product doesn't exist or is too small to be worthy of pursuit.

Second, you should conduct a preliminary patent search on your own to see if your idea is already patented. You can do this by going to the United States Patent & Trademark Office (USPTO) Web site (www.uspto.gov/) and conducting a preliminary search. Just for fun, try this example. Suppose you invented a toothbrush with a tube of toothpaste attached to the handle. Go to the USPTO Web site, locate the Search text box at the top of the pages, and type "toothbrush + toothpaste." You'll find that 265 patents have already been granted for devices that in various ways combine toothbrushes and toothpaste. While you may find a new way to combine toothbrushes and toothpaste, and be granted a patent, you hardly have a completely original idea. In fact, patent # 6390103 is titled "Toothpaste Dispensing Toothbrush Having Floss Dispenser."[1] This patent, which was granted in 2002, goes one step further than you were thinking.[2]

> You should test and screen your business idea to make sure it has value in the marketplace.

None of this is to suggest that you shouldn't apply for a patent if you've invented a new device, but just be careful. The costs involved, which vary depending on the complexity of the device, range from between $4,500 to $6,500 to patent a relatively simple device, like a new type of paper clip, to between $6,500 and $9,000 to patent a moderately complex device, like a retractable dog leash. The costs involved include attorney fees and United States Patent & Trademark Office filing fees. Costs go up substantially when trying to patent a highly complex product like a new type of medical device.[3]

The costs involved include attorney fees and United States Patent & Trademark Office filing fees.

What is a patent, and what's eligible for patent protection?

A patent is a grant from the federal government conferring the rights to exclude others from making, selling, or using an invention for the term of a patent. However, a patent does not give its owner the right to make, use, or sell the invention; it gives the owner only the right to exclude others from doing so. This is a confusing issue for many people. If a business is granted a patent for an item, it is natural to assume that it could start making and selling the item immediately. But it cannot. A patent owner can legally make or sell the invention only if no other patents are infringed on by doing so. For example, if an inventor obtained a patent on a computer chip and the chip needed technology patented earlier by Intel to work, the inventor would need permission from Intel to make and sell the chip. Intel may refuse permission or ask for a licensing fee for the use of its patented technology. Although this system seems odd, it is really the only way the system could work. Many inventions are improvements on existing inventions, and the system allows for improvements to be patented, but only with the permission of the original inventors, who usually benefit by obtaining licensing income in exchange for their consent.

There are three types of patents: utility patents, design patents, and plant patents. Utility patents are the most common type of patent and cover what we generally think of as new inventions. The term of a utility patent is 20 years from the date of the initial application. After 20 years, the patent (which is not renewable) expires, and the invention falls into the public domain. A complete description of the invention for which a utility patent is sought is required, including drawings and technical details. A patent must be applied for within one year of when a product or process was offered for sale, put into public use, or described in any printed publication—or the right to file a patent application is forfeited. There are three basic requirements for a patent to be granted. The subject of the patent application must be (1) useful, (2) novel in relation to prior arts in the field, and (3) not obvious to a person of ordinary skill in the field.

Provisional patent applications

One provision of patent law that is particularly critical to small business owners is that the U.S. Patent and Trademark Office (USPTO) allows inventors to file a provisional patent application, pending the preparation and filing of a complete application. Filing for a provisional patent allows the term "Patent Pending" to be applied to an invention. Filing for a provisional patent grants "provisional rights" to an inventor for up to one year, pending the filing of a complete and final application.

TRUTH

35

Trademarks: An essential form of protection

Unlike patents, nearly all small businesses can benefit from trademark protection. Once the name, logo, and other distinguishing marks for a business have been selected, they should be trademarked so they become the sole possession of the business's owner.

What is a trademark?

A trademark is any word, name, symbol, or device used to identify the source or origin of products or services and to distinguish those products or services from others.

> Nearly all small businesses can benefit from trademark protection.

Archaeologists have found that as far back as 3,500 years ago, potters made distinctive marks on their articles of pottery to distinguish their work from others. As discussed in Truth 17, "Something you'll say a million times: Your business's name," the name (and other marks) a business associates with itself makes a difference in terms of how it's perceived and whether it gets noticed. For example, the original name that Jerry Yang and David Filo, the cofounders of Yahoo!, selected for their business was "Jerry's Guide to the World Wide Web." Not too catchy, is it? The name was later changed to Yahoo!, which caught on with early adopters of the Internet and is now one of the most recognizable trademarks in the world.

There are four types of trademarks: trademarks, service marks, collective marks, and certification marks. Trademarks and service marks are of the greatest interest to business owners. Service marks are similar to trademarks, but they are used to identify the services or intangible activities of a business rather than a business's physical product. Travelocity, eBay, and Google are examples of service marks.

How a trademark is obtained

Trademarks are obtained through the United States Patent & Trademark Office (USPTO) and are renewable every ten years, as long as the mark remains in use. Once you've selected a trademark, you should conduct a trademark search to determine if the trademark is available. If someone else has already established rights to the proposed mark, you can't use it. You also can't choose a trademark that is confusingly similar to someone else's trademark. For example, if you tried to trademark the name Apple Core for a computer company, Apple Inc. would undoubtedly argue that your name is confusingly similar to its name.

Technically, a trademark does not have to be registered to receive protection and to prevent other companies from using confusingly similar marks. Once a mark is used in commerce, such as in an advertisement, it is protected. There are distinct advantages, however, to registering the mark through the USPTO. Registered marks are allowed nationwide priority for use of the mark, are permitted to use the federal trademark registration symbol (®), and carry with them the right to block the importation of infringing goods into the United States. The right to use the registered trademark symbol is particularly important. Attaching a trademark symbol to a product (for example, My Yahoo!®) provides notice of a trademark owner's registration. This posting allows an owner to recover damages in an infringement action and reduces an offender's claim that it didn't know that a particular name or logo was trademarked.

You can register a trademark on your own. In fact, there are a number of Web sites, including the USPTO site, that provide step-by-step instructions for how to register a trademark. There are gray areas in trademark law, however, and you want to get it right. You also don't want to infringe on someone else's trademark. Accordingly, in most cases, it's advisable to retain an attorney to help you secure your trademarks.

What can be trademarked?

The following items are eligible for trademark protection:

- Words, such as Yahoo! and Microsoft
- Numbers and letters, such as 3M, CNN, and 1-800-CONTACTS
- Designs and logos, such as the Nike swoosh logo
- Sounds, such as the familiar four-tone sound that accompanies "Intel Inside" commercials

- Fragrances, such as the special scent on certain brands of stationary
- Shapes, such as the distinctive shape of the Apple iPod
- Colors, such as the distinctive purple color of Nexium, a pill that treats acid reflux disease (advertised as the "purple pill")
- Trade Dress, such as the distinctive appearance of the inside of a Panera Bread restaurant

Trademark protection is broad and provides many opportunities for businesses to differentiate themselves from one another. The key for a new business is to trademark its products and services in ways that draw positive attention to them.

Rules of thumb for selecting appropriate trademarks

There are two rules of thumb to help businesses owners select appropriate trademarks. First, a mark, whether it is a name, logo, or design, should display creativity and strength. Marks that are inherently distinctive, such as the McDonald's Golden Arches; made-up words, such as Google and eBay; and words that evoke particular images, such as Double Delight Ice Cream; are strong trademarks.

Second, words that create favorable impressions about a product or service are helpful. A name such as Safe and Secure Childcare for a day care center positively resonates with parents.

TRUTH

36

Copyrights laws:
A surprising breadth
of protection

Of all the forms of intellectual property protection, the copyright laws are possibly the least understood. Most of us think of books, newspaper articles, and musical scores as needing copyright protection. But copyright law extends much further. Nearly anything that a business creates that is in written or digital form is eligible for copyright protection.

A copyright is a form of intellectual property protection that grants to the owner of a work of authorship the legal right to determine how the work is used and to obtain the economic benefits from it.[1] The work must be in tangible form, such as a book or computer software program. Businesses typically possess a treasure trove of copyrightable material. A work does not have to have artistic merit to be eligible for copyright protection. As a result, things such as operating manuals and advertising brochures qualify for protection.

> Businesses typically possess a treasure trove of copyrightable material.

What is protected by a copyright?

Copyright law protects "original works of authorship." The primary categories of material that can be copyrighted are as follows:

- Literary works
- Musical compositions
- Computer software
- Dramatic works
- Sound recordings
- Architectural works
- Motion pictures and other audiovisual works
- Pictorial, graphic, and sculptural works

Anything that is written down is a *literary work*. Characters that are associated with a company qualify for protection. A character that looks like the Aflac duck or the GEICO gecko would infringe on the copyright that protects those characters. *Derivative works*, which are works that are new renditions of something that is already copyrighted, are also copyrightable. As a result of this provision, a musician who performs a rendition of a song copyrighted by Aerosmith can obtain a copyright on his or her effort. Of course, Aerosmith would have to consent to the infringement on its copyright of the original song before the new song could be used commercially, which is a common way that composers and bands earn an extra income.

The main exclusion from copyright law is that a copyright cannot protect an idea. For example, a business owner may have the idea to open a soccer-themed restaurant. The idea itself is not eligible for copyright protection. However, if the business owner writes down what the soccer-themed restaurant will look like and how it will operate, that description is copyrightable.

> The main exclusion from copyright law is that copyrights cannot protect ideas.

How to obtain a copyright

Technically, a copyright exists the moment a work of authorship assumes a tangible form. You have to register the copyright with the U.S. Copyright Office (www.copyright.gov), however, if you want to bring a lawsuit for infringement. There are two steps that are normally taken to solidify a copyright, cumulating with registering a work with the copyright office.

First, you can enhance copyright protection for anything in written form by attaching the copyright notice, or *copyright bug* as it is sometimes called. The bug—a C inside a circle—typically appears in the following form: © 2008 Kitchen Sentry Inc. By placing this notice at the bottom of a document, an author (or company) can prevent people from copying the work without permission and claiming that they did not know that the work was copyrighted. Substitutions for the copyright bug include the word Copyright and the abbreviation *Copr.*

Second, you can obtain further protection by registering the work with the U.S. Copyright Office. Filing a simple form and depositing one or two samples of the work with the office completes the registration process. The need to supply a sample obviously depends on the nature of the item involved. Obviously, you could not supply one or two copies of an original painting. Filing promptly is recommended and makes it easier to sue for copyright infringement if necessary.

Copyrights last for a long time. Any work created on or after January 1, 1978, is protected for the life of the author plus 70 years.

Copyright infringement

Copyright infringement occurs when one work derives from another or is an exact copy or shows substantial similarity to the original work. It is a growing problem in the United States and in other countries. For example, less than a week after the original *Harry Potter* movie was released in the United States, bootleg video discs were reported for sale in at least two Asian countries.[2] To prove infringement, a copyright owner is required to show that the alleged infringer had prior access to the copyrighted work, and the work is substantially similar to the owner's.

There are many ways to prevent infringement. For example, a technique frequently used to guard against the illegal copying of software code is to embed and hide in the code useless information, such as the birth dates of the authors. It's hard for infringers to spot useless information if they are simply cutting and pasting large amounts of code from one program to another. If software code is illegally copied and an infringement suit is filed, it's difficult for the accused party to explain why (supposedly original) code includes the birth dates of its accusers. Similarly, some publishers of maps and other reference works deliberately include bits of phony information in their products, such as fake streets and nonexistent railroad crossings, to try to capture copiers. Again, it would be pretty hard for someone who copied someone else's copyrighted street guide to explain why the name of a fake street was included.[3]

TRUTH

37

Trade secrets: Guard them carefully

Most businesses, including start-ups, have a wealth of information that is critical to their success but does not qualify for patent, trademark, or copyright protection. Some of this information needs to be kept secret to help a business maintain its competitive advantage. An example is a business's customer list. A business may have been extremely diligent over time tracking the preferences of its customers, helping it fine-tune its marketing message and target past customers for future business. If this list fell into the hands of one or more of the company's competitors, its value would be diminished, and it would no longer provide the company a unique competitive advantage.

A trade secret is any formula, pattern, physical device, idea, process, or other information that provides the owner of the information with a competitive advantage in the marketplace. Trade secrets include marketing plans, product formulas, financial forecasts, employee rosters, logs of sales calls, and similar material. Unlike patents, trademarks, and copyrights, there is no single government agency that regulates trade secret law. Instead, the theft of trade secrets is made illegal by a patchwork of state and federal economic espionage laws.

> Trade secrets include marketing plans, product formulas, financial forecasts, employee rosters, logs of sales calls, and similar material.

What qualifies for trade secret protection?

Not all information qualifies for trade secret protection. In general, information that is known to the public or that competitors can discover through legal means doesn't qualify for trade secret protection. If a company passes out brochures at a trade show that are available to anyone in attendance, nothing in the brochure can typically qualify as a trade secret. Similarly, if a secret is disclosed by mistake, it typically loses its trade secret status. For example, if an employee of a business is talking on a cell phone in a public place and is overheard by a competitor, anything the employee says is generally exempt from trade secret protection. Simply stated, the general philosophy of trade secret legislation is that the law does not protect a trade secret unless the owner has protected it first.

Businesses can maintain protection for their trade secrets if they take reasonable steps to keep the information confidential. The strongest case for trade secret protection is information that is characterized by the following:

- Is not known outside the company
- Is known only inside the company on a "need-to-know" basis
- Is safeguarded by stringent efforts to keep the information secret
- Is valuable and provides the company a competitive advantage
- Was developed at considerable cost, time, and effort
- Cannot be easily duplicated, reverse-engineered, or discovered

Trade secret disputes

Trade secret disputes arise most frequently when an employee leaves a business to join a competitor and is accused of taking confidential information along. For example, a marketing manager for one business may take a job with a competitor and create a marketing plan for the new employer that is nearly identical to the plan being worked on at the previous job. The original employer could argue that the marketing plan that the departed employee was working on was a company trade secret and that the employee essentially stole the plan and took it to the new job. The key factor in winning a trade secret dispute is that some type of theft must have taken place. Trade secrets can be lawfully discovered. For example, it's not illegal for one company to buy another company's products and take them apart to see how they're assembled.

Trade secret disputes arise most frequently when an employee leaves a business to join a competitor and is accused of taking confidential information along.

A company damaged by trade secret theft can initiate a civil action for damages in court. In denying the allegation, the defendant typically argues that the information in question was independently developed (meaning that no theft took place), was obtained by proper means (such as with the permission of the owner), or was innocently received (such as through a casual conversation at a business meeting). Memorization is not a defense. An employee from one business can't say, "All I took from my old job was what's in my head" and claim that just because the information conveyed wasn't in written form, it's not subject to trade secret protection. If the courts rule in favor of the business that feels one of its trade secrets has been stolen, the firm can stop the offender from using the trade secret and obtain substantial financial damages.

The best way to protect trade secrets is through physical measures and written agreements. Physical measures range from placing security fences around buildings to restricting access to sensitive files like customer lists. Written agreements are also key. For the best protection, a business should ask its employees to a sign a nondisclosure agreement at the time of original employment. A *nondisclosure agreement* is a promise by an employee or another party (such as a supplier) not to disclose a company's trade secrets.

How to approach marketing in a new business

Marketing refers to all the activities that a business engages in to be successful in selling a product or service that people not only desire but are willing to buy.[1] Most of a business's marketing activities are executed through one of the four Ps of the marketing mix—product, price, promotion, and place (or distribution). Most new business owners see the development of an effective marketing program as a key factor to their ultimate success.

Be careful, however, of how you think about marketing and the financial resources that you dedicate to it. Marketing is one area where hard work and ingenuity can make up for a lack of funds. It's also an area where money can be easily wasted if a business doesn't have a well-thought-out marketing plan. There are three things to be mindful of as you approach the topic of marketing and promotions in a new business.

Make your marketing efforts consistent with your mission

First, a business's marketing efforts should be consistent with its overall mission and values. For example, Kitchen Sentry, the fictitious firm introduced in Truth 33, "Intellectual property: What is it, and how is it protected?", has the mission of protecting individuals and families against kitchen fires. The company believes that people fear kitchen fires as much as any calamity that might befall themselves or their families, and that having a high-quality smoke alarm in the kitchen will provide people peace of mind. Kitchen Sentry's marketing efforts should reflect and reinforce these core beliefs. A common mistake that new businesses make is that their marketing efforts are poorly focused. Stay on script. If the people behind Kitchen Sentry care deeply about protecting families from kitchen fires and their product is sound, those attributes should be the focal points of the company's marketing efforts.

Know your customers

Second, a business needs to have a clear sense of who its customers are and how they behave. A well-managed start-up uses a two-step approach for selecting its market: segmenting the market and selecting or developing a target market. This process is explained in Truth 39, "Segmenting the market and selecting a target market." A business must complete these steps and clearly define who its customers are, because all of its marketing decisions hinge on these initial critical choices. If other marketing decisions are made first, such as choosing an advertising campaign, there is a danger the firm will not send a clear message to its target customers. For example, if a jewelry store that features high-end merchandise advertised in a local shopper alongside discount merchants, it would risk sending confusing signals to its intended market. It's more affluent clientele might wonder, "Is this a high-end store, or isn't it?"

It's also important that a business knows as much about its customers as possible, from knowing the amount of disposable income they have, to the periodicals they read, to the media they watch. Knowledge of these and similar factors helps you fine-tune your marketing strategy and lower expenses.

Learn about the full array of marketing techniques that are available

Third, a business needs to learn about the full array of marketing techniques that are available. The majority of business owners are familiar with the most expensive ways to run a marketing campaign, such as buying print and media advertising, but they are less familiar with more cost-efficient alternatives. Many of the most cost-effective ways for a business to get noticed, from passing out brochures to speaking to civic groups, are inexpensive but take time and effort. The best approaches to learning about the methods available are to look through books and magazines on marketing and promotions and take a class from your local Small Business Development Center (SBDC).

An example of an inexpensive way for a business to get noticed is to write a blog. Blogs familiarize people with a business and help build an emotional bond between a business and its customers. A case in point is a blog written by Mary Baker, the co-owner of Dover Canyon Winery. Baker started her blog in April 2006 using a software package called TypePad Pro that costs her $149.50 a year to maintain. She uses the blog to give her readers periodic updates on what's happening at the winery and how she feels about her life and her business. She also posts pictures of herself, her pets, her family, and daily life at the winery. To make her customers aware of her blog, she drops a postcard with the blog's address into bags with customer purchases. There is also a link to the blog on the Dover Canyon Winery's Web site. Mail order sales for the winery almost doubled from 2006 to 2007.[2]

While writing a blog may not be appropriate for all businesses, the overarching point is that Mary Baker found an inexpensive and novel way to promote her business, rather than relying on more traditional and expensive forms of promotion. In a midsized city, a large newspaper ad can run as high as $5,000.

39

Segmenting the market and selecting a target market

A new business must address this critical question: Who are our customers, and how will we appeal to them? A well-managed start-up uses a two-step approach to answer the first of these questions: segmenting the market, and selecting or developing a specific target market.

Segmenting the market

The first step in selecting a target market is to study the industry in which your firm intends to compete and determine the different potential target markets in that industry. This process is called market segmentation. Market segmentation is important because a new business generally has only enough resources to target one market segment, at least initially.[1] Markets can be segmented in many ways, such as by geography (city, state, country), demographic variables (age, gender, family income), psychographic variables (personality, lifestyle, values), and benefits sought (quality, ease of use, prestige). Sometimes a business segments its market on more than one dimension to drill down to a specific market segment that the business thinks it is uniquely capable of serving. For example, GreatCall, the company that makes Jitterbug, a cell phone designed specifically for older people, segmented the cell phone market by age and by benefits sought. The Jitterbug, which targets older users, features large buttons, easy-to-read text, and a cushion that cups around the ear to improve sound quality. Similarly, PopCap games, an electronics games company, segmented its industry by gender and benefits sought. It targets women and makes electronic games that are casual and relaxing. This is an entirely different segment from the segment targeted by Electronic Arts, the largest company in the electronic games industry. Electronic Arts targets young males and produces games that are flashy and action-packed.

> Market segmentation is important because a new business generally has only enough resources to target one market segment, at least initially.

To test whether you have segmented your market successfully, the requirements for successful market segmentation are as follows:

- Uniformity of needs and wants appears within the segment.
- Diversity of needs and wants exists between the segments.
- Differences within the segment should be small compared to differences across segments.
- The segment should be distinct enough so that its members can be easily identified.
- It should be possible to determine the size of the segment.
- The segment should be large enough to be profitable.

Despite the importance of market segmentation, it is a process that new businesses often overlook. Overlooking this activity can result in a business that hasn't carefully studied the possibilities in the industry it plans to enter before selecting its target market. One opportunity that new businesses have is to segment their markets in new ways. Before Great Call and PopCap Games came along, no one had segmented the cell phone market by age and benefits sought or segmented the electronic games industry by gender and type of game. Both of these companies now have growing businesses, largely because they are servicing distinct and growing segments within their broader industries.

Selecting a target market

Once a firm has determined the different markets that exist within an industry, the next step is to select a target market. Typically, a new business doesn't target an entire segment of a market, because many market segments are too large to target successfully. Instead, most businesses target a smaller niche or vertical market within the segment (as discussed in Truth 8, "A make-it or break-it issue: Selecting an idea that can be sold into a niche market"). For example, one segment of the fitness industry is fitness centers that sell monthly memberships. (Another segment would be companies that sell exercise equipment to be used in the home.) Within the segment that sells monthly membership are several smaller niche markets that are targeted by different companies. For example, Curves targets women, Cuts targets men, My Gym is just for children, and Club 50 targets people 50 years old and older.

By focusing on a clearly defined target market, a business can become an expert in that market and then be able to provide customers with high levels of value and service.

In most cases, the secret to appealing to a smaller niche market is to understand the market and meet its needs better than those needs can be met by businesses targeting an entire market segment. This is the secret behind the phenomenal success of Curves, which grew from one fitness center for women in 1992 to over 10,000 today.[2] By focusing on a clearly defined target market, a business can become an expert in that market and then provide customers with high levels of value and service. This advantage is one of the reasons that Philip Kotler, a world-renowned marketing expert, says, "There are riches in niches."[3]

TRUTH

40

Establishing a brand

A brand is a set of attributes that people associate with a business. These attributes can be positive, such as trustworthy, innovative, dependable, or easy to deal with, or they can be negative, such as cheap, unreliable, sloppy, or difficult to deal with.

The customer loyalty a company creates through its brand is one of its most valuable assets. This sentiment is affirmed by Russell Hanlin, the CEO of Sunkist Growers, who said, "An orange is an orange...is an orange. Unless...that orange happens to be a Sunkist, a name 80 percent of consumers know and trust."[1] By putting its name on an orange, Sunkist is making a promise to its customers that the orange will be wholesome and fresh. Other ways of thinking about the meaning of a brand are as follows:

- A brand is a guarantee.
- A brand is a pledge.
- A brand is a reputation.
- A brand is an unwritten warrantee.
- A brand is an expectation of performance.
- A brand is a presentation of credentials.
- A brand is a collection of memories.
- A brand is a handshake between a company and its customers.

Start-ups must build a brand from scratch, which starts with selecting the company's name. One of the keys to effective branding is to create a strong personality for a business, designed to appeal to the chosen target market.[2] Southwest Airlines, for example, has created a brand that denotes fun. This is a good fit for its target market: people traveling for pleasure rather than for business. Similarly, Starbucks has created a brand that denotes an experience framed around warmth and hospitality, encouraging people to linger and buy additional products. A business ultimately wants its customers to strongly identify with it—to see themselves as "Southwest Airlines flyers" or "Starbucks coffee drinkers." People won't do this, however, unless

> The customer loyalty a company creates through its brand is one of its most valuable assets.

158

they see a company as being different from competitors in ways that are significant to them.

So how does a new business develop a brand? On a philosophical level, a business must have meaning in its customers' lives. It must create value—something that customers are willing to pay for. Imagine a father shopping for airline tickets so that he can take his three kids to see their grandparents for Christmas. If Southwest Airlines can get his family to their destination for $75 per ticket cheaper than its competitors, Southwest has real meaning in the father's life. Similarly, if a young couple buys a Cranium board game, and playing the game with other couples results in lasting friendships, Cranium will have a special place in their hearts. Businesses that create meaning in their customers' lives stand for something in terms of benefits, whether it is low prices, fun, fashion, improved health, or something else.

On a more practical level, brands are built through a number of techniques, including advertising, public relations, sponsorships, support of social causes, and good performance. A business's name, logo, Web site design, and even its letterhead are part of its brand. A new business needs to think about the brand it plans to develop before it picks its logo and initiates other marketing-related activities. The first impression a business makes with its potential customers should convey the essence of how it wants to be viewed and seen.

Affirming all these points, Dan Byrne, the CEO of Byrne Specialty Gases, a company that provides specialized gases to laboratories, sums up what his company has done to build a strong brand during its 20 years of existence:

> A business's name, logo, Web site design, and even its letterhead are part of its brand.

"It is all based on trust, reliability, responsiveness, quality, etc. It is all these infinitesimal details that drive a company's brand. We have the attitude that everything matters. We lost a large customer once that went to a discount provider. Three months later the customer called back almost hat in hand. Our level of service reinforces our brand and keeps customers coming back to us."[3]

TRUTH

41

Selling benefits rather than features

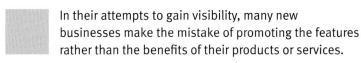

In their attempts to gain visibility, many new businesses make the mistake of promoting the features rather than the benefits of their products or services.

A promotional strategy that focuses on the features of a product, such as its technical merits, is almost always less effective than a strategy that focuses on what a product can do for the person buying it. For example, one of the most successful advertising campaigns ever launched by McDonald's featured the jingle, "You deserve a break today—at McDonald's." McDonald's could have stressed the cleanliness of its stores or the uniformity of its French fries, which are features. Instead, it struck a chord with people by focusing on one of the biggest benefits of eating at McDonald's—not having to cook. Although not as obvious in today's society, not having to cook a meal at home was a rare treat when McDonald's started using this tagline.

The same rationale can be applied to any product or service. Consider the ZUCA rolling backpack (introduced in Truth 32). In her initial attempts to get the ZUCA noticed, Laura Udall, the company's founder, could have talked about the ZUCA's durable aluminum frame, its oversized silent wheels, its washable nature, and its number of available colors. All these are features. But it's more likely that she focused on the benefits of the product—the fact that it relieves back pain and is durable enough that a child can sit on it while waiting for the school bus. (The ZUCA includes a fold-out seat.) These are the benefits or the value that the ZUCA delivers to its users.

Sometimes it's hard to resist the temptation to focus on features rather than benefits. For instance, it's easy to imagine why an engineer who has just invented a new product wants to talk about the product's technical specifications. Similarly, it's natural for a company that has just developed an improved digital camera to want to point out all the bells and whistles that its camera has that other cameras don't. However, one of the most fundamental precepts of marketing is that "customers don't buy features; they buy benefits."[1] The first thing that customers want to know is how the product or service will help them accomplish their goals and improve their lives.

TRUTH

42

Pricing:
The most dicey element in
the marketing mix

Of the four elements of a business's marketing mix—product, price, promotion, and place (or distribution), price is often the toughest. A business doesn't want to undercharge for its products and services and leave money on the table, nor does it want to overcharge and drive business away.

The price a company charges for its products and services also sends a clear message to its target market. For example, Oakley positions its sunglasses as innovative, state-of-the art products that are both high quality and visually appealing. This position in the market suggests the premium price that Oakley charges. If Oakley advertised innovative, state-of-the art products but charged a bargain basement price, it would send confusing signals to its customers. Its customers would wonder, "Are Oakley sunglasses high quality, or aren't they?" In addition, the lower price wouldn't generate the sales revenue Oakley needs to continuously differentiate its sunglasses from competitors' products in ways that are meaningful to its customers.

> The price a company charges for its products and services sends a clear message to its target market.

Most business owners use one of two methods to set the price for their products: cost-based pricing and value-based pricing.

Cost-based pricing

In cost-based pricing, the list price is determined by adding a markup percentage to a product's cost. The markup percentage may be standard for the industry or may be arbitrarily determined by the business owner. The advantage of this method is that it is straightforward, and it is relatively easy to justify the price of a product or service. The disadvantage is that it's not always easy to estimate what the costs of a product will be, particularly for a start-up. Once a price is set, it is difficult to raise it, even if a company's costs increase. In addition, cost-based pricing is based on what a company thinks it should receive rather than on what the market thinks a product or service is worth. It is becoming increasingly difficult for businesses to dictate prices to their customers, given customers' ability to comparison-shop on the Internet and find what they believe is the best bargain for a product.[1]

Value-based pricing

In value-based pricing, the list price is determined by estimating what customers are willing to pay for a product and then backing off a bit to provide a cushion. What a customer is willing to pay is determined by the perceived value of the product and by the number of choices available in the marketplace. Sometimes, to make this determination, a business has to conduct focus groups or try different pricing options to test markets. A business influences its customer's perception of value through branding, promotions, and the other elements of its marketing mix.

Whether you choose cost-based pricing or value-based pricing is an important call. Most experts recommend value-based pricing because it hinges on the perceived value of a product or service rather than a cost plus markup, which is a formula that ignores the customer.[2] Most experts also warn new business owners to resist the temptation to charge a low price for their products in the hopes of capturing market share. This approach can win a sale but generates little profit. In addition, most consumers make what's called a price-quality attribution when looking at the price of a product. This means that consumers naturally assume that the higher-priced product is also the better-quality product.[3] If a business charges a low price for its products, it sends a signal to its customers that the product is low quality regardless of whether it really is.

> Most experts recommend value-based pricing because it hinges on the perceived value of a product or service rather than a cost plus markup, which is a formula that ignores the customer.

Of course, regardless of whether a business chooses cost-based or value-based pricing, its price must make sense given the realities of the marketplace. Some businesses are able to charge a premium price for their product or service. To charge a premium price, one or more of the following characteristics must generally be present:

- Demand for the product is strong relative to supply.
- Demand for the product is inelastic. (People will buy at almost any price.)
- The product is patent protected and has a clearly defined target market.
- The product offers additional features that produce tangible benefits (for example, a strong warranty that protects against having to prematurely replace the product).
- A new technology is being introduced.
- The product serves a compelling need (like a pharmaceutical product that relieves pain).
- The product is a luxury item and targets an affluent clientele.

TRUTH

43

It's okay to advertise, but think through your choices carefully

There are many ways that businesses advertise. While it's normally cost-prohibitive for new businesses to advertise on television and in major newspapers and magazines, there are alternatives that are less expensive or free. Pick and choose carefully. Advertising is an area where a business can spend a lot of money to produce meager results, or spend very little and achieve impressive outcomes.

The two major categories of advertising include print and media advertising and Internet advertising.

> Advertising is an area where a business can spend a lot of money to produce meager results, or spend very little and achieve impressive outcomes.

Print and media advertising

Print and media advertising runs the gamut from television ads to posting flyers on grocery store bulletin boards. The type of advertising a business selects hinges largely on whether it's targeting a national audience or a local clientele. There are some advertising-related initiatives that all new businesses should take advantage of. For example, the major search engines, like Google and Yahoo!, have business directories that list local businesses and, in some cases, even provide a map to show where they are located. You can get your business listed but have to go to the Web sites and sign up. The listings are either free or subject to a small yearly fee. If you want to see how this works, type "sporting goods stores in Tulsa, Oklahoma" into the Google search bar and see what happens. The names of the "local businesses" that appear have registered their businesses in the Google business directory.

Radio advertising is effective for many businesses that have a local station with a listening audience that reflects the demographic they're trying to reach. Classified ads, either in local newspapers or online, remain effective in many instances. Direct mail, placing an ad in a local business directory, and advertising in publications such as local homeowners' association newsletters are additional choices. A business's own signage and visibility can be its most effective form of advertising. Some home remodeling businesses, for example, report that their top source for getting new business is people who see their trucks parked in neighborhoods and call the phone number displayed on the side of the trucks.

Another option is to advertise in an industry trade journal. A trade journal is a periodical, magazine, or publication that focuses on a specific industry, trade, or type of business. A directory of trade associations (which publish trade journals) is available through Weddle's.[1] Many trade associations also sponsor trade shows and conferences where new businesses can gain visibility and display their products.

Internet advertising

An increasingly effective way for new businesses to get noticed and sell their products is via pay-per-click Internet advertising, as discussed in Truth 15, "Internet businesses: The sky does seem to be the limit." This type of advertising is provided by the major search engines, such as Google, Yahoo!, and MSN. Google has two pay-per-click programs—AdWords and AdSense. AdWords allows an advertiser to buy keywords on Google's home page, which triggers text-based ads to the side (and sometimes above) the search results when the keyword is used. If you type "watches" into the Google search bar, you see ads from businesses that sell watches. Many companies report impressive results utilizing this approach, presumably because they are able to place their ads in front of people who are already searching for information about their products. Google's other pay-per-click program is called AdSense. It is similar to AdWords, except the advertiser's ads appear on other Web sites or blogs instead of Google's home page. You've seen AdSense ads many times as you've looked at Web sites and blogs. They are easy to spot because they have a small emblem underneath the ads that says, "Ads by Google."

> An increasingly effective way for new businesses to get noticed and sell their products is via pay-per-click Internet advertising.

TRUTH

4

Public relations:
More important than ever

One of the most cost-effective ways for a new business to get noticed and to promote its product or service is through public relations. Public relations refer to efforts to establish and maintain a positive image for a company with the public.

The major difference between public relations and advertising is that public relations efforts are not paid for—directly. The cost of public relations to a business is whatever it takes to network with journalists and other people to try to interest them in saying and writing good things about a company and its products. While there is nothing inherently wrong with advertising and similar forms of promotion, people know that ads and promotions are paid for, so they discount them to a certain degree. It's normally more persuasive when an unbiased third party talks about the merits of your product or service.[1] The key to getting good public relations, such as a newspaper or magazine article written about your company, is to create a human interest story that's associated with your business. It also helps to be proactive in regard to speaking out on behalf of your industry and talking to trade groups and civic groups about your area of expertise.

> The key to getting good public relations, such as a newspaper or magazine article written about your company, is to create a human interest story that's associated with your business.

There are other ways in which a business can enhance its chances of getting public relationship via the press. One technique is to prepare a press kit, which is a folder that contains background information about the company and includes a list of its most recent accomplishments. The kit is normally distributed to journalists and is placed on the business's Web site. In fact, if you've ever picked up a national magazine and read an article about a business in a small town and wondered how the magazine knew about the business, it's typically because the business sent the magazine a press kit and the business's story (or product or service) fit the article the magazine was interested in writing about.

Another way to generate public relations is to win an award or be recognized in some positive manner. For example, in 2007, WhiteWave's Silk Soymilk won the American Culinary ChefsBest Award for the Best Taste. WhiteWave can now refer to the award in its promotions and has earned the right to display the ChefsBest seal of approval on its products.[2]

Another way to generate public relations is to win an award or be recognized in some positive manner.

Businesses also generate public relations by attending trade shows and similar events. For example, the largest trade show for consumer electronics is International CES, which is held in Las Vegas every January. Many new technology firms use this show to present their products to the public for the first time. They do this in part because they have a captive media audience that is eager to find interesting stories to write about.

There are also community- and industry-related activities that a business owner can engage in to generate positive public relations for the firm. Examples include writing a column in a local newspaper, publishing a company newsletter, and speaking to civic groups. These activities cost little or no money but can enhance the image of a business.

A representative list of public relations activities include

- Press releases
- Media coverage
- Articles about the business in local newspapers, national magazines, or industry press
- Blogging
- Monthly newsletter
- Sponsoring free seminars
- Contributing expert how-to or advice articles in your local newspaper
- Civic, social, and community involvement

TRUTH

45

Distribution and sales:
More choices than ever

Distribution encompasses all the activities that move a business's products from its place of origin to the consumer. For some businesses, like restaurants and fitness centers, distribution is not a major issue because they service their customers directly. But for many companies, like Kitchen Sentry, the smoke detector company introduced in Truth 38, "How to approach marketing in a new business," the landscape is much different. Kitchen Sentry will have key decisions to make regarding how its products will be distributed and sold.

Distribution and sales alternatives

The first step in determining a distribution and sales strategy is to sort through the choices. For example, imagine you are starting a business that sells hardware products to consumers. You could opt to field a sales force that approaches retail chains like Home Depot and Lowe's to persuade them to carry your products. You could sell directly to consumers without the need for salespeople, through catalog or Internet sales. Another option is to sell through an intermediary, such as a distributor, wholesaler, or manufacturer's representative. If you decided to go this route, your intermediary would call on Home Depot and Lowe's on your behalf. Intermediaries are sometimes difficult to find and attract. It's not uncommon for a firm to have to "prove" that its product will sell, by selling it itself, before a high-quality distributor or wholesaler will sign on.

> The first step in determining a distribution and sales strategy is to sort through the choices.

Similar choices apply for some service businesses. Hotels, for example, sell their services (typically rooms) directly through their Web sites and telephone reservation services and through intermediaries, such as travel agents, tour operators, and airlines. For example, if you were planning a trip to Walt Disney World in Orlando, Florida, you could book your flight, rental car, and hotel through Orbitz, Expedia, or many similar services. In these cases, Orbitz and the others are acting as intermediaries for the service providers.

The key to making the right choices among these alternatives is to think carefully first about where people in your target market shop, and then about the most effective and economical way to get your products some shelf space in those outlets. You also need to think about the operational ramifications of your choices. Although it might sound good to get your product placed in Wal-Mart or Costco from the outset, few new businesses are prepared to ramp up production fast enough or offer the huge volume of product needed to satisfy these types of retailers. In addition, you need to carefully weigh the choice of retail outlets and other resellers with your brand and the image you want to convey to your target market. Coach, for example, is a billion-dollar company that sells stylish handbags, footwear, and accessories. It's built its business by selling through specialty stores rather than mass merchandisers. Specialty stores are more consistent with Coach's upscale image than mass merchandisers; they appeal to consumers who prioritize quality and brand image over price.

Sales strategy and related issues

If you decide to employ your own sales force, you'll need to decide how many salespeople will be needed, how the numbers will be ramped up as the company grows, and how the salespeople will be compensated. These factors vary by industry, so you'll probably need to talk to industry experts and study industry trade journals to make these calls.

If you decide to distribute your products through intermediaries, you'll have to decide how the intermediaries will be chosen and the ways in which the intermediaries will interface with the sales outlets in your industry. In most cases, you'll have to support your distributors and wholesalers with training, technical support, shipping, point-of-sale advertising material, and other forms of sales support.

An exciting element of distribution and sales strategy for new businesses is that you don't always have to follow the conventional forms of distribution and sales. One way a business can innovate and provide unique value in the marketplace is through distribution and sales. For example, Dell revolutionized the computer industry by deciding to sell directly to consumers rather than through retail

An exciting element of distribution and sales strategy for new businesses is that you don't always have to follow the conventional forms of distribution and sales.

stores. Similarly, ProFlowers is making noise in the flower industry by changing the number of hands that flowers pass through before they are sold to consumers. Flowers are raised by growers and then typically pass through the hands of an importer (or distributor), wholesaler, and retailer before they are sold to the customer. This process typically takes between 7 and 12 days. As a flower passes through the process, temperature and humidity often change, which degrades the flower's appearance and shortens its vase life.

ProFlowers, which sells online, has sharply reduced the number of steps a flower must go through as it travels from the grower to the customer. When an order is placed via its Web site, ProFlowers routes the order to a grower that it has contracted with. The grower fills the order and ships it directly to the customer via UPS or FedEx utilizing proprietary technology provided by ProFlowers. The intermediaries are eliminated, saving ProFlowers money and allowing the customer to receive flowers that are fresher and last longer than flowers purchased through a traditional outlet.

46

Managing a business's finances

A business owner's ability to get a business up and running and to keep the business operating smoothly hinges largely on prudent financial management. Regardless of the quality of a product or service or how compelling of a need it fills, a company can't be viable in the long run unless it is successful financially.

There are many practical issues involved in the prudent financial management of a business. A business owner must be aware of how much money the business has in the bank and if that amount is sufficient to satisfy the business's financial obligations. Just because a business is successful doesn't mean that it doesn't face financial challenges. For example, many small businesses that sell their products to larger companies, such as Motorola, 3M, and Home Depot, don't get paid for 30 to 60 days from the time they make a sale. Think about the difficulty this scenario creates. The small firm must buy parts, pay its employees, pay its routine bills, ship its products, and wait for one to two months for payment. Unless a business manages its money extremely carefully, it is easy to run out of cash, even if its products or services are selling like hotcakes. Similarly, as a company grows, its cash demands often increase to service a growing clientele. A business needs to accurately anticipate whether it will be able to fund its growth through earnings or if it will need to establish a line of credit at a bank or look for investment capital.

> Just because a business is successful doesn't mean that it doesn't face financial challenges.

The financial management of a business deals with questions such as the following on an ongoing basis:

- How are we doing? Are we making or losing money?
- How much cash do we have on hand?
- Do we have enough cash to meet our short-term obligations?
- How efficiently are we utilizing our assets?

- How do our growth and net profits compare to those of our industry peers?

- Where will the funds we need for capital improvements come from?

- Are there ways we can partner with other firms to share risk and reduce the amount of cash we need?

- Overall, are we in good shape financially?

A properly managed business stays on top of the issues suggested by these questions through the tools and techniques discussed in Truth 47, "Financial objectives of a business," and Truth 48, "The nitty-gritty: Forecasts, budgets, and financial statements."

Particularly important issues for first-time business owners

First-time business owners need to be aware of two additional issues that play a role in financial management.

First, many businesses are viable and ongoing once they get started. The trick is to get them started. Unless your business is cash flow positive from the beginning, which is rare, there will be a period when you'll lose money while you're ramping up the business. For example, you may be planning to open a fitness center and have determined that you'll make money if you can sign up 1,200 or more members. But you won't have 1,200 members the day you open. It may take you six months to a year to reach your membership goal. In the meantime, all your fixed expenses (and most of your variable expenses) will march on. Most businesses do experience a start-up period during which they lose money (or make little money) until they are fully up to speed and reach profitability. Businesses need to be fully aware that this period will take place and to plan for it. The worst time to go to a bank, family member, or investor to help meet a cash shortfall is when you're facing a cash crisis.

> Many businesses are viable and ongoing once they get started. The trick is to get them started.

The second thing to be mindful of if you are a first-time business owner is that most people are not familiar with how to complete the types of forecasts, budgets, and financial statements that are needed to prudently manage the finances of a growing business. If you fall into this category (as most people do), don't wing it. Get help. The financial management of a business is too imperative not to take it seriously. A good source for one-on-one help is SCORE, an organization mentioned several times in this book. Small Business Develop Centers (SBDCs) frequently hold workshops on how to complete financial statements and learn accounting and budgeting software programs.

TRUTH
47

Financial objectives of a business

Before a business develops the types of forecasts, budgets, and financial statements that it needs to manage its finances, it must have a firm grasp of its financial objectives. Nearly all businesses have three main financial objectives: profitability, liquidity, and overall financial stability. Understanding these objectives sets a business on the right financial course and helps explain the need for forecasts, budgets, and financial statements, which will be discussed in Truth 48, "The nitty-gritty: Forecasts, budgets, and financial statements."

> Nearly all businesses have three main financial objectives: profitability, liquidity, and overall financial stability.

Profitability

Profitability is the ability to earn a profit. Many start-ups are not profitable their first several months of operations, as discussed in Truth 47, "Financial objectives of a business," but they must become profitable to create a sustainable business and provide a return to their owners.

A business also must know if its profits are increasing or declining and whether they are leading or lagging industry averages. The first question, whether a business's profits are increasing or declining, can be answered through the maintenance of accurate financial records. The second question, whether a business's profits are leading or lagging industry averages, is tougher. Normally, businesses collect this information through informal conversations with industry peers or by joining an industry trade group, which typically collects information about the average profitability for businesses in the industry.

Obviously, if a business's profits are declining (or are nonexistent) or if the business is lagging industry averages, corrective action is necessary. One thing that continually surprises small business counselors is the number of small business people who don't have a good grasp on whether their profits are increasing or declining and how they stack up against their industry peers. Don't fall into that group. Stay on top of these issues so you can take corrective action immediately if necessary.

Liquidity

Liquidity is a company's ability to meet its short-term financial obligations. As indicated in Truth 46, "Managing a business's finances," a business must carefully manage its cash to make sure it has enough money in the bank to meet its payroll and cover its short-term obligations.

Normally, the biggest culprits in straining a business's liquidity are letting its accounts receivables or its inventory levels get too high. There are many colorful anecdotes about business owners who have had to rush to a bank and get a second mortgage on their houses to cover their business's payroll. This set of events usually occurs when a business takes on too much work and its customers are slow to pay. A business can literally have a million dollars in accounts receivable but not be able to meet a $25,000 payroll. This is why almost any book you pick up about growing a business stresses the importance of properly managing your cash flow.

Some businesses deal with potential cash flow shortfalls by establishing a line of credit at a bank or by maintaining a healthy cash reserve. Other businesses are careful not to take on too much work, so their accounts receivable and inventory levels remain manageable.

Overall financial stability

Stability is the strength and vigor of the business's overall financial posture. For a business to be stable, it must not only earn a profit and remain liquid but also keep its debt in check. If a firm continues to borrow from its lenders and its debt-to-asset ratio (which is calculated by dividing its total debt by its total assets) gets too high, it may have trouble meeting its obligations and securing the level of financing needed to fuel its growth.

Many business owners are caught off guard by the continuing need to remain vigilant regarding the overall financial stability of their business. You would think that if a business got off to a good

Many business owners are caught off guard by the continuing need to remain vigilant regarding the overall financial stability of their business.

start, increased its sales, and started making money, things would get progressively more stable. In many instances, however, just the opposite happens. Imagine the following scenario. A business gets off to a fast start and projects that its sales will double in the next two to three years. To make this happen, the business needs more people and additional equipment to handle the increased workload. The new equipment needs to be purchased, and the new people need to be hired and trained before the increased business generates additional income. Even though the business might be better off in the long run as a result of the increased business, it's easy to see the strain that's placed on the business in the short run to get there.

TRUTH

48

The nitty-gritty: Forecasts, budgets, and financial statements

To assess whether its financial objectives are being met, businesses rely heavily on the preparation and the ongoing analysis of forecasts, budgets, and financial statements. In addition, it's necessary for business owners to learn basic bookkeeping, to keep their records straight for tax and other reporting purposes.

Forecasts

A forecast is an estimate of a business's future income and expenses. It's the first step in completing a budget and a set of projected (or pro-forma) financial statements. A business that is already up and running bases its forecasts on its past performance, its current circumstances, and its future plans. So a business that grossed $250,000 last year would use that figure as a starting point for projecting next year's sales and would then adjust the figure upward or downward based on current circumstances (that is, state of the economy, entrance of new competitors, buying mood of customers) and future plans. The same rationale applies for forecasting expenses.

It's harder to forecast the initial sales and expenses for a start-up. There are four common ways to go about it:

- Contact the trade associations in your industry to ask if they track the annual sales and expense numbers for businesses that are similar to the one you plan to start.

- Find a comparable business and ask the owner if he or she would help you predict your initial sales and expenses.

- Conduct Internet searches to see if you can find articles about businesses that are similar to the one you plan to start. Occasionally, the articles will include sales and expense figures.

- Utilize the multiplication method to project sales. If you're planning to sell a product on a national basis, like the Kitchen Sentry Smoke Detector, utilize a top-down approach: You estimate the total number of people who buy smoke detectors, estimate the average price they pay, and then estimate the percentage of the market you believe you will get. If you have a business that will sell on a local basis, like a restaurant or a clothing boutique, you utilize a bottom-up approach: You determine how many customers to expect and the average amount each one will spend.

Most experts feel that finding a business comparable to the one you plan to start and asking the owner for input is the most effective method for forecasting the initial sales and expenses for a new business.

Most experts feel that finding a business comparable to the one you plan to start and asking the owner for input is the most effective method for forecasting the initial sales and expenses for a new business.

Budgets

Budgets utilize the information generated by forecasts and organize a business's income and expenses into specific categories. In most cases, a business completes its forecasts and budgets simultaneously. Organizing a business's income and expenses into specific categories provides a practical way of tracking those numbers on an ongoing basis and helps a business answer the question, "Are we on track financially?"

Budgets also help a business in day-to-day decision making. For example, if a business budgets $10,000 a year for marketing, and midyear it has spent $5,000 of its budget, it knows that it can't say yes to an advertising company that is trying to persuade it to buy a $7,500 marketing campaign for the remainder of the year without exceeding its budget.

Financial statements

To further understand, track, and document their financial performance, businesses should also complete historical and projected financial statements on a regular basis. The statements include the income statement, balance sheet, and cash flow.

The historical income statement reflects the results of the operators for a business for a given period. It records all the projected sales and expenses and shows whether the business is making a profit or is experiencing a loss. The balance sheet is a snapshot of a business's assets, liabilities, and owner's equity at a specific point in time. It is an important tool for measuring a business's overall financial stability. The cash flow shows the money that is flowing into and the money that is flowing out of a business on an ongoing basis; it provides a real-time picture of a business's cash position. Projected financial statements are similar to historical statements except they look forward rather than backward.

Completing both historical and projected financial statements takes some practice, and most business owners buy books, attend workshops, or work with their accountants to learn how to prepare the statements. If you aspire to obtain a bank loan, seek investment capital, or sell your business at some point, you need to maintain accurate financial statements. It's difficult for a banker, investor, or potential buyer to analyze your business without historical and projected incomes statements, balance sheets, and cash flows to go by.

TRUTH

49

Preparing for growth

Most businesses want to grow. Even businesses that are started to accommodate a certain lifestyle or allow their owner to meet a personal goal or aspiration normally want to expand their sales and profits over time.

Growth doesn't happen by chance, however. Growing a business successfully takes preparation, good management, and an awareness of the challenges involved. Growing a business can be a joy or a nightmare—trust me, I've seen both. There are many businesses that have started, grown prudently, and are thriving, returning to their owners just the sort of lives they had hoped for. Sadly, there are also many businesses that have done just the opposite—they've started, grown either too slowly or too quickly, and have failed, leaving their owners financially and emotionally drained.

> Growing a business successfully takes preparation, good management, and an awareness of the challenges involved.

The key to properly preparing for growth involves appreciating the nature of growth and planning for it in a conscientious and purposeful manner.

Appreciating the nature of business growth

There are two central things to appreciate about the nature of business growth. First, not all businesses have the potential to be aggressive growth firms. The businesses that have the potential to grow the fastest over a sustained period of time are ones that solve a significant problem or have a major impact on their customers' productivity or lives. This is why the lists of fast-growing businesses are often dominated by technology and health-care companies. These companies have the potential to make the biggest impact on their customer's lives. This point is affirmed by comparing the frozen food industry to medical products and biotechnology. In 2007, the frozen food industry grew by 0.6 percent, while the medical products industry grew by 3.2 percent and biotechnology grew by 9.5 percent.[1] While there is nothing wrong with starting a business in frozen foods, you need to have a realistic outlook on how fast the business will likely grow. Even though an individual frozen food company may get off to a fast start, as it gets larger, its annual growth will normally start to reflect its industry's norms.

The second thing that a business owner needs to appreciate about growth is that a business can grow too fast. Many businesses start fast and never let up, which is stressful for everyone involved. Other businesses start, grow at a measurable pace, and then experience a sudden upswing in orders and have difficulty keeping up. This scenario can transform a business with satisfied customers and employees into a chaotic workplace with people working 50+ hours a week scrabbling to push the business's product out the door as quickly as possible. Here are some indicators that a business is growing too fast:

- You have to borrow money to pay for routine operating expenses.
- You have extremely tight profit margins.
- You have an overstretched staff.
- Your quality is slipping.
- Customer complaints are up.
- Your productivity is falling.
- The work environment is stressful and frantic.

The way to prevent these and similar outcomes from happening is to recognize when to put the brakes on and have the courage to do it. Sometimes this means actually turning down business, which can be a hard thing to do for a business that is committed to servicing its customers in the best manner possible.

Planning for growth

You also should plan for growth. The process of writing a business plan, discussed in Truth 10, "Writing a business plan: Still as important as ever," greatly assists in this effort. A business plan normally includes a detailed forecast of a business's first three to five years of sales along with an operations plan that describes how the business will meet its forecasts. Even though the business will invariably change during the first three to five years, it's good to have a plan. Many businesses periodically revise their business plans and allow them to help guide their growth-related decisions.

A business owner should also step back and measure the business's growth plans against his or her personal goals and

A business owner should also step back and measure the business's growth plans against his or her personal goals and expectations.

expectations. As mentioned in Truth 2, "The right business for you," a decision to grow quickly will necessitate a quick pace of activity and a hectic lifestyle. Although the upside may be a more financially successful business, sacrifices will have to be made in terms of the number of hours worked and the pressures that accompany a more hectic lifestyle.

50

Stages of growth: More opportunities, more challenges

The majority of businesses go through a discernible set of stages referred to as the organizational life cycle. These stages include introduction, early growth, continuous growth, maturity, and decline. Each stage must be managed differently. Business owners need to be familiar with these stages, along with the unique opportunities and challenges that each stage entails.

The introduction, early growth, and continuous growth stages are focused on here.

Introduction

This is the start-up phase where a business determines what its core strengths and capabilities are and starts selling its initial products or services. It's a hands-on phase for the owner, who is normally involved in every aspect of the day-to-day operations of the business. The business is typically nonbureaucratic, with no (or few) written rules or procedures. The main goal of the business is to get off to a good start and to try to gain momentum in the marketplace.

The primary challenges for a business in the introduction stage are to make sure the initial product or service is right and to start laying the groundwork for building a larger and busier organization. Don't rush things. For instance, if you start a Web site to sell shoes, it's normally best to make sure your approach to selling shoes works and resonates in the marketplace before adding handbags, sunglasses, and other items.

> The primary challenges for a business in the introduction stage are to make sure the initial product or service is right and to start laying the groundwork for building a larger and busier organization.

In regard to laying the groundwork to build a larger organization, many businesses use the introduction stage to try different concepts to see what works and what doesn't, recognizing that trial and error gets harder as the business grows. It's good to document what works and start thinking about how the business's success can be replicated when the owner isn't present or when the business expands beyond its original location.

Early growth

A business's early growth stage is characterized by increasing sales and heightened complexity. The business is normally still focused on its initial product or service but is trying to increase its market share and might have related products in the works. The initial formation of policies and procedures takes place, and the process of running the business starts to consume more of the owner's time and attention.

For a business to be successful in this stage, two things must take place. First, the owner of the business must start transitioning from his or her role as the hands-on-supervisor of every aspect of the business to a more managerial role. As articulated by Michael E. Gerber in his excellent book *The E-Myth Revisited*, the owner must start working "on the business" rather than "in the business."[1] The basic idea is that early in the life of the business, the owner is typically directly involved in building the product or delivering the service that the business provides. As the business moves into the early growth stage, the owner must let go of that role and spend more time learning how to manage and build the business. If the owner isn't willing to make this transition or doesn't know that it needs to be made, the business will never grow beyond the owner's ability to directly supervise everything that takes place, and the business's growth will eventually stall.

The second thing that must take place for a business to be successful in the early growth stage is that increased formalization must take place. The business has to start developing policies and procedures that tell employees how to run it when the owner or other top managers aren't present. This is how a McDonald's restaurant runs so well when it's staffed by what appears to be a group of teenagers. The employees are simply following the policies and procedures that were originally written down by Ray Kroc, McDonald's founder, and have been added to and improved over the years. An early growth stage business will not develop policies and procedures as elaborate as McDonald's, but it must start formalizing how it achieves its success.

Continuous growth stage

As a business moves beyond its early growth stage and its pace of growth accelerates, the need for structure and formalization increases. The resource requirements of the business are usually a major concern, along with the ability of the owner and manager to take the firm to the next level. Often, the business will start developing new products and services and will expand to new markets. Smaller firms may be acquired, and the business might start partnering with other firms.

The importance of developing policies and procedures increases during the continuous growth stage. A business also needs to develop a formal organizational structure and determine clear lines of delegation throughout the business. Although *formalization* is a term that is often frowned upon by business owners who want to free themselves from the trappings of Corporate America, well-developed policies and procedures lead to order, which typically makes the process of growing a business more organized, enjoyable, and successful.

> The importance of developing policies and procedures increases during the continuous growth stage.

TRUTH

51

Strategies for growth

The practical side of growth is the actual strategies that businesses employ to grow their organizations. It's helpful for business owners to be acquainted with the breadth of growth-related strategies that are available so they can select the strategy or strategies that make the most sense at a certain point in time in light of their individual situations.

The strategies for growth are divided into internal growth strategies and external growth strategies.

Internal growth strategies

Internal growth strategies involve efforts taken within the business, such as new product development, other product-related strategies, and international expansion. Almost all businesses start by featuring internal growth, and many businesses stick with this strategy as they grow. Here are the most common internal growth strategies:

- New product development
- Improving an existing product or service
- Increasing the market penetration of an existing product or service
- Extending product lines
- Geographic expansion
- International expansion

Many businesses prefer internal growth because it typically leads to an incremental, even-paced approach to growth. For example, many retailers start with one store and then grow by opening additional stores or by selling their products through distributors. By growing in this manner, the company can control its pace of growth and time its store openings and new distribution agreements to coincide with the resources it has available. It's also easier for a business to control its culture by growing through internal means. If a business grows by adding employees as new products (or stores) come online, it can socialize the employees into its culture. Conversely, if a firm grows via an external strategy, such as an acquisition, it will have employees who have been raised in different corporate cultures and will normally have a more difficult time creating cohesion among its employees.

The primary downside of internal growth is that it tends to be a slow form of business growth. While a slow, deliberate approach to growth has many advantages, in some industries relying strictly on internal growth does not permit a business to develop sufficient economies of scale or broaden its product offerings fast enough to remain competitive.

Almost all businesses start by featuring internal growth, and many businesses stick with this strategy as they grow.

External growth strategies

External growth strategies rely on establishing relationships with other firms, such as mergers, acquisitions, strategic alliances, and franchising. It is increasingly common for businesses to utilize one or more external growth strategies as soon as the early growth stage of its organizational life cycle. Here are the most common external growth strategies:

- Merger
- Acquisition
- Licensing agreement
- Strategic alliance
- Joint venture
- Franchising

A business can normally grow faster through external growth than internal growth because it immediately adds a product or capability that might have taken months or years to develop internally. For example, when eBay acquired PayPal, it acquired PayPal's proprietary electronic payments system, something PayPal worked diligently to perfect over a period of several years. Similarly, by forming a strategic alliance or joint venture, a firm can tap into the resources of its partner and reach new markets without having to build out its

A business can normally grow faster through external growth than internal growth because it immediately adds a product or capability that might have taken months or years to develop internally.

own infrastructure. For example, many American food companies have strategic alliances with large European food companies to gain access to their European distribution networks.

The primary downside of external growth is that by relying on other firms to help develop its growth, a business loses some of its flexibility and decision autonomy. It also complicates its business and runs the risk of joining with a partner that is either unreliable or doesn't share its core values. The net result of engaging in external growth is usually to speed up a business's pace of growth. As a business's pace of growth increases, the challenges of growth, such as cash flow management, are usually exacerbated.

Many businesses blend internal and external strategies for growth as they pass through the stages of growth and expand their businesses. The important thing to remember as a business owner is that you should select the means of growth that is best for you and your company, given the conditions you face and the lifestyle decisions you've made.

TRUTH

52

Work life balance:
Practical tips

Most people start businesses to improve their lives—whether the goal is to make more money, have a more flexible lifestyle, or pursue a particular passion. But business ownership can also be all-consuming. It can easily consume the majority of a person's time and attention and negatively affect an individual's marriage, family life, and physical and emotional well-being.

Fortunately, there are steps that business owners can take to strike a healthy balance between their business and their personal lives, but there is a catch. The catch is that the steps must actually be taken—they can't just be thought about or put on a to-do list. The following is a list of three practical tips for starting a business and maintaining a healthy personal life. Candidly, it's been my observation that people who start businesses and end up with miserable personal lives don't do any of these things. Don't let this happen to you. Take these tips to heart, and search for additional tips and advice.

Establish a routine

Many business owners suffer because they don't place boundaries on their business life. The enviable result is working long hours because there is always something that needs to be done. The way to solve this problem is to set a routine and stick to it. Depending on the nature of your business, you could set your hours for 8:00 a.m. to 5:00 p.m. on weekdays. If that isn't a realistic approach, you could commit to being home every evening by 6:00 p.m. or commit to not working on Saturdays and Sundays.

> Many business owners suffer because they don't place boundaries on their business life.

While you'll have to find a schedule that works for you, the overarching point is to establish a routine and stick to it. This approach will provide you time to unwind and will allow your family to reliably schedule activities during your free time.

Get help

There is no reason to "go it alone" as a business owner. Virtually every city and midsized town has an active SCORE chapter, and access to Small Business Development Centers and other sources of counseling and advice are either available or just a stone's throw away. You should also align yourself with mentors and set up a board of advisors, as suggested in Truth 32, "Board of advisors." The ability to share the pressures of your business with others relieves burnout and typically leads to a brighter and healthier disposition. As your business grows, you may also be able to shift some of the pressure to partners or employees.

An example of the positive influence that a mentor or advisor can have is provided by Oron Strauss, a business owner who received funding from a business angel. Recalling an experience with his angel investor, Strauss said,

> "About a year ago, when I was having a particularly bad week, I fired off a long, heartfelt e-mail message to my angel. I explained, in great detail, the difficulties I faced and my thoughts about them. His response was succinct: 'All sounds normal. You're handling it well. Keep up the good work.' My first response was disappointment over what struck me as a curt response. Then I realized that the angel had given me the best possible response. He understood what I was going through was normal and that I would make it."[1]

Imagine how advice like this positively affects a person's personality disposition and self-esteem. One of the best ways to maintain a successful business and a healthy personal life is to remain emotionally healthy yourself.

One of the best ways to maintain a successful business and a healthy personal life is to remain emotionally healthy yourself.

Set up systems and procedures

A third way to find the right balance between your business and your personal life is to put in place systems and procedures that help the business run without your being physically present. This is a step that takes time and experience to implement but is vital. One of the worst predicaments to get into, as a business owner, is to open a restaurant, store, or similar business and base so much of the success of the business on your physical presence that you feel you can't leave while the business is open. This type of setup traps a business owner into a life of long hours, week after week, with no end in sight. It's hard for anyone to run a successful business and maintain a healthy personal life under these types of circumstances.

A much better approach is to carefully document every aspect of how the business is run and then develop systems, policies, and procedures that others can follow while you aren't physically present. This scenario is what allows a business to run smoothly and reflect all the positive attributes of the owner, even when the owner isn't physically present. It's also the only way a business owner can maintain a normal life, especially if the business is open 70 to 80 hours a week, which is normal for a restaurant or retail store.

TRUTH

53

Starting a business as a means of achieving a healthy personal life

While many business owners start businesses and then struggle to find the right balance between their business and their personal life, others approach the process in the opposite manner. They begin with a desire to achieve a properly balanced life and then start a business as a means of achieving it.

There are three distinct advantages that business ownership offers in regard to achieving a healthy personal life. These advantages are available in varying degrees, depending on the nature of the business. In some cases, they represent the very reason that people choose business ownership over a traditional career.

Flexibility

Although most business owners work just as hard or harder than people in traditional jobs, they normally have more flexibility in their schedules. This facet of business ownership appeals to people who feel strongly about goals that they have outside of work, like being home when their kids get off the school bus or doing volunteer work. Some people value this facet of business ownership so much that they're willing to sacrifice some level of income for self-employment. This sentiment is affirmed by Margot James, a business owner who wrote,

> "One of the reasons I enjoy what I do is the flexibility. I have other interests besides paid work. I do a lot of volunteer community work...I have decided that whatever needs I have, I could sacrifice some level of income for flexibility. I made that conscious decision."[1]

Being your own boss also provides you the flexibility to build a business that is consistent with your personal values and ideas. For example, Chick-fil-A, a $2 billion chain of chicken restaurants, isn't open on Sundays and places books and other "values-based" messages in its kids meals. These practices are a direct reflection of founder Truett Cathy's personal values.

Achieving a personal goal or aspiration

As indicated in Truth 1, "Why people start businesses," sometimes starting a business is the only way people can fulfill their most important goals and aspirations. For example, there are heartfelt stories of people who have faced challenges in their lives, such as a child with a debilitating medical issue, who have had to create businesses to find a solution for their child's problem because no other solution was available. In these instances, a person's goals and aspirations quickly shift to finding relief for a loved one's suffering or affliction.

Although most business owners work just as hard as or harder than people in traditional jobs, they normally have more flexibility in their schedules.

Other examples are less extreme but demonstrate a similar point. One example is Sue Schwaderer and Bill Lawrence. In the late 1990s, Schwaderer was making a six-figure income working for Oracle Software, and Lawrence was successful managing three apartment buildings they owned in Evanston, Illinois, a Chicago suburb. Although they were making good money, they didn't enjoy their everyday life. "We were tired of never seeing each other and of too much business travel...too much traffic, too many people, too much noise," Schwaderer recalls.[2] The two left their life in Chicago behind and opened a 14-room bed and breakfast in picturesque Saugatuck, Michigan, a town of 1,000. Although the income from the bed and breakfast doesn't match what they were making in Chicago, they are happier and enjoy the less hectic pace of a smaller town.

The ability to pursue a passion

Finally, as expressed throughout this book, the ability to pursue a personal passion is the instrumental reason that many people start their own business. In many instances, the business returns to the owner a sense of fulfillment and satisfaction that has a positive impact on his or her personal life.

REFERENCES

Truth 1

1 Low, Murray B., and I. C. MacMillian. 1988. Entrepreneurship: Past research and future challenges. *Journal of Management.* Vol. 14, No. 2: 139–161.

2 Lee, J. and S. Venkataraman. 2006. Aspirations, market offerings, and the pursuit of entrepreneurial opportunities. *Journal of Business Venturing.* 21: 107–123.

3 Kruger, N. F. Jr., M. D. Reilly, and A. L. Carsrud. 2000. Competing models of entrepreneurial intentions. *Journal of Business Venturing.* 15: 411–432.

Truth 2

1 Pervin, L. A. 1968. Performance and satisfaction as a function of individual-environment fit. *Psychology Bulletin.* 26: 56–68.

2 Berry, T. Mirror, mirror, on the wall: What startup? Up and running blog. http://upandrunning.entrepreneur.com. (accessed March 1, 2008).

3 PricewaterhouseCoopers. 2001. *Three keys to obtaining venture capital.* New York: PricewaterhouseCoopers.

Truth 3

1 Vivarelli, M. 2004. Are all potential entrepreneurs so good? *Small Business Economics.* 23: 41–49.

Truth 4

1 Smilor, R. W. 1997. Entrepreneurship reflections on a subversive activity. *Journal of Business Venturing.* 12: 341–346.

2 Bunder, S. 1962. Intolerance of ambiguity as a personality variable. *Journal of Personality* (Volume 30): 29–50.

3 Bandura, A. 1997. *Self-efficacy: The exercise of control.* New York: Freeman.

4 Gist, M., and T. Mitchell. 1992. Self-efficacy: A theoretical analysis of its determinants and malleability. *Academy of Management Review.* 17: 183–211.

Truth 5

1 Direct Sales Association home page. www.dsa.org (accessed March 16, 2008).

Truth 6

1 Cooper. S., and others. December 2006. The hot list. Entrepreneur.com.

2 Darlin, D. February 3, 2006. The iPod ecosystem. *The New York Times.*

Truth 7

1 Rietzschel, E. F., B. A. Nijstad, and W. Stroebe. 2006. Productivity is not enough: A comparison of interactive and nominal brainstorming groups on idea generation and selection. *Journal of Experimental Social Psychology.* 42: 244–251.

2 Rodan, K. April 2006. Entrepreneurial thought leaders. Podcast, Stanford Technology Ventures, http://stvp.stanford.edu.

Truth 8

1 "500 List." January 2004. Inc., 64.

Truth 9

1 Mullins, J. W. 2003. *The new business road test.* London: Prentice-Hall.

2 Goel, S., and R. Karri. 2006. Entrepreneurs, effectual logic, and over-trust. *Entrepreneurship Theory and Practice.* 30: 477–493.

Truth 10

1 Shane, S., and F. Delmar. 2004. Planning for the market: Business planning before marketing and the continuation of organizing efforts. *Journal of Business Venturing.* 19: 767–785.

2 Honig, B., and T. Karlsson. 2004. Institutional forces and the written business plan. *Journal of Management.* Vol. 30, No. 1: 29–48.

3 Barringer, B. 2009. *Preparing effective business plans.* Upper Saddle River, New Jersey: Prentice-Hall.

4 www.score.org/index.html

Truth 11

1 "How much money does it take to start a small business?" August 15, 2006. *Wells Fargo/Gallup Small Business Index*. San Francisco: Wells Fargo Bank.

2 "Inc 500." 2006. *Inc.* Special Issue.

Truth 12

1 "Learning curves." *Franchise Times.*, www.franchisetimes.com/content/story.php?article=00303 (accessed April 10, 2008).

2 Prince, C. J. Buying balance by finding a franchise. Success Magazine. www.successmagazine.com/article.php?article_id=195 (accessed April 10, 2008).

Truth 13

1 Direct Sales Association home page. www.dsa.org (assessed April 8, 2008).

2 Ibid.

3 The Pampered Chef home page. www.pamperedchef.com (accessed April 8, 2008).

4 Christopher, D. 2005. *The pampered chef.* New York: Doubleday: ix.

Truth 14

1 Dahl, D. April 2008. The most valuable companies in America. *Inc.*: 99.

2 Harper, S. 2003. *Starting your own business.* New York: McGraw-Hill.

Truth 16

1 McLinden, S. June 2006. Who's afraid of the giant? *Shopping Center Today.* www.icsc.org/srch/sct/scto606/cozy_walmart.php (accessed October 2, 2007).

2 Ballou, J., et al. 2008. *The Kauffman firm study.* Kansas City: The Kauffman Foundation.

Truth 19

1 Shane, S. 2008. *The illusions of entrepreneurship.* New Haven, Connecticut: Yale University Press.

2 Ballou, J., et al. 2008. *The Kauffman firm study.* Kansas City: The Kauffman Foundation.

Truth 20

1 Lally, J. August 30, 2006. Building an online store. *Small Business Technology Magazine.* 10.

2 This information is adapted from Karess, V. Guide to creating a Web site. Work.com Web site. www.work.com/creating-a-web-site-936/ (accessed April 4, 2008).

3 King, R. February 26, 2007. No geeks required. *BusinessWeek.*

Truth 21

1 Shane, S. 2008. *The illusions of entrepreneurship.* New Haven, Connecticut: Yale University Press.

2 Livingston, J. 2008. *Founders as work: Stories of startups' early days.* New York: Apress, p. 259.

3 Ladies Who Launch home page. www.ladieswholaunch.com (accessed April 27, 2008).

Truth 23

1 Shane, S. 2008. *The illusions of entrepreneurship.* New Haven Connecticut: Yale.

2 Minniti, M., and W. Bygrave. 2005. *Global entrepreneurship monitor 2003 executive report.* Babson Park, MA: Babson College and London Business School.

3 Ebben, J., and A. Johnson. 2006. Bootstrapping in small firms: An empirical analysis of change over time. *Journal of Business Venturing* (in press).

Truth 24

1 Ballou, J., et al. 2008. *The Kauffman firm survey.* Kansas City: The Kauffman Foundation.

2 Marlow, S., and D. Patton. 2005. All credit to men? Entrepreneurship, finance, and gender. *Entrepreneurship Theory & Practice.* 29: 717–735.

3 Prosper home page. www.prosper.com (accessed April 26, 2008).

4 Count Me In home page. www.countmein.org/site/ (accessed April 26, 2008).

5 Make Mine a Million $ Business home page. www.
makemineamillion.org (accessed April 27, 2008).

6 Accion USA home page. www.accionusa.org/site/c.lvKVL9MUIsG/
b.1359227/k.55A6/Small_Business_Loans__Microlending.htm
(accessed April 27, 2008).

Truth 25

1 Melloan, J. July 2005. Angels with angels. *Inc.*

2 Ibid.

Truth 26

1 Nance-Nash, S. May 2005. Seeking seed money: Grants for starting
a small business are available through a variety of local sources.
Here's how to get them. *Black Enterprise.*

Truth 27

1 Visa Business Breakthrough Contest home page. http://
businessbreakthrough.msn.com (accessed April 27, 2008).

2 Vermont Community Loan Fund home page. www.vclf.org (accessed
April 27, 2008).

3 First Community Loan Fund home page. www.firststateloan.org
(accessed April 28, 2008).

4 Patriot Express Pilot Loan Initiative home page. www.sba.gov/
patriotexpress (accessed April 29, 2008).

5 Minority Business Development Agency home page. www.mbda.
gov (accessed April 29, 2008).

6 Minority Angel Investor Network. www.fundingpost.com/
angelgroup/angel-group-profile.asp?fund=72 (accessed April 29,
2008).

Truth 28

1 Read, C., et al. 2001. eCFO. Chichester, UK: John Wiley & Sons, p. 117.

Truth 29

1 Fesser, H., and G. Willard. 1990. Founding strategy and performance:
A comparison of high and low growth tech firms. *Strategic
Management Journal.* Vol. 11, No. 2: 87–98.

2 Moray, N. and B. Clarysee. 2004. A process study of entrepreneurial team formation: The case of a research-based spin-off. *Journal of Business Venturing.* 19: 55–79.

3 Forbes, D., et al. 2006. Entrepreneurial team formation: An exploration of new member additions. *Entrepreneurship Theory & Practice.* 30: 225–248.

4 Eisenhardt, K., and C. Schoonhoven. 1990. Organizational growth: Linking founding team, strategy, environment, and growth among U.S. semiconductor ventures, 1978–1988. *Administrative Science Quarterly.* 35: 504–529.

5 Zenger, T. and B. Lawrence. 1989. Organizational demography: The differential effects of age and tenure distribution of technical communication. *Academy of Management Journal.* 32: 353–376.

6 *Black's Law Dictionary.* 2002.

Truth 30

1 PricewaterhouseCoopers. June 7, 2006. Fast-growth CEOs more optimistic, but increasingly concerned about availability of qualified workers and pressure for increased wages, PricewaterhouseCoopers finds. *Trendsetter Barometer.* Council of Entrepreneurial Development. Entrepreneurial satisfaction survey report. 2004. Raleigh-Durham, North Carolina.

2 IRS Small Business Web site. www.irs.gov/businesses/small (accessed May 8, 2008).

Truth 31

1 Jaffe, D., and P. Levensohn. November, 2003. After the term sheet: How venture boards influence the success or failure of technology companies. White paper. Levensohn Venture Partners. www.levp.com (accessed May 6, 2008).

2 Busenitz, L., J. Fiet, and D. Mosel. 2005. Singling in venture capitalist-new venture team funding decisions: Does it indicate long-term venture outcomes? *Entrepreneurship Theory and Practice.* 29: 1–12.

Truth 32

1 Sherman, A. 2001. *Fast-track business growth.* Washington, DC: Kiplinger Books.

2 Featured mom inventors: Laura Udall. Mom Inventors home page. www.mominventors.com (accessed May 6, 2008).

3 Coolibar home page. www.coolibar.com (accessed May 6, 2008).

4 Intouch Health home page. www.intouchhealth.com (accessed May 6, 2008).

Truth 34

1 USPTO home page. www.uspto.gov (accessed May 10, 2008).

2 United States Patent & Trademark home page. www.uspto.gov (accessed May 9, 2008).

3 Quinn, G. Costs of obtaining a patent. IPWatchdog home page. www.ipowatchdog.com (accessed May 10, 2008).

Truth 36

1 Bagley, C., and C. Dauchy. 2003. *The entrepreneur's guide to business law*, 2nd edition. Florence, KY: Cengage Learning.

2 *Los Angeles Times.* November 20, 2001.

3 Wired. November 11, 2005.

Truth 38

1 Wikipedia. Marketing. http://en.wikipedia.org/wiki/Marketing (accessed May 21, 2008).

2 Tram the grapes, write the blog. August/September 2007. *Business Week SmallBiz*, p. 72.

Truth 39

1 Weinstein, A. 2006. A strategic framework for defining and segmenting markets. *Journal of Strategic Marketing.* Vol. 14, No. 2: 115–127.

2 Curves home page. www.curves.com (accessed May 27, 2008).

3 Kother, P. 2003. *Marketing insights from A to Z.* New York: John Wiley & Sons, p. 65.

Truth 40

1 Kother, P. 2003. *Marketing insights from A to Z.* New York: John Wiley & Sons, p. 65.

2 Seybold, P. B. 2001. *The customer revolution.* New York: Crown Business.

3 Kaiser, N. C. Dan Byrne, CEO of Byrne Specialty Gases. nPost.com (www.npost.com), from the manuscript of an interview conducted April 29, 2004.

Truth 41

1 Lodish, L. M., H. L. Morgan, and A. Kallianpur. 2001. *Entrepreneurial marketing*. New York: John Wiley & Sons.

Truth 42

1 Silverstein, M. J. 2006. *Treasure hunt*. New York: Portfolio.

2 Boyett, J. H. and J. T. Boyett. 2003. T*he guru guide to marketing*. New York: John Wiley & Sons.

3 Foster, T. 2001. *Managing quality*. Upper Saddle River, New Jersey: Prentice-Hall.

Truth 43

1 Weddle's home page. www.weddles.com (accessed May 28, 2008).

Truth 44

1 Ries, A., and L. Ries. 2003. *The fall of advertising and the rise of PR*. New York: HarperCollins.

2 Silk Soymilk home page. www.silksoymilk.com (accessed May 28, 2008).

Truth 49

1 IBISWorld. 2008.

Truth 50

1 Gerber, M. E. 2004. *The e-myth revisited*. New York: HarperCollins.

Truth 52

1 Strauss, O. Touched by an angel. *Entrepreneur's byline*. www. entreworld.org (accessed March 20, 2003).

Truth 53

1 Davies, S. 2000. *Gender capital: Entrepreneurial women in American society*. New York: Taylor & Francis, p. 124.

2 Henricks, M. May 29, 2002. Freedom, not money, drives these startups. *The Wall Street Journal*.

For my family, Janet, John, Jennifer, and Emily.

About the Author

Bruce Barringer, a renowned expert on entrepreneurship, is Professor of Management at University of Central Florida. His books include *Entrepreneurship: Successfully Launching New Ventures, 2nd Edition, Preparing Effective Business Plans: An Entrepreneurial Approach*, and *What's Stopping You?: Shatter the 9 Most Common Myths Keeping You from Starting Your Own Business.*